A Different Kind of Childhood

Jean Jupe

ISBN No: 978.1.906542.26.9

Publishers: Barny Books
               Hough on the Hill
               Grantham
               Lincolnshire
               NG32 2BB

               Tel: 01400 250246
               www.barnybooks.biz

Printers: Peter Spiegl & Co
               42 Guash Way
               Ryhall Road Industrial Estate
               Stamford
               Lincolnshire
               PE9 1XH

               Tel: 01780 762550
               www.spiegl.co.uk

Cover illustrated by Roger McKay

Acknowledgements

Watford Museum for research in particular Lindsay Hayward, Sarah Pennington
The British library in particular Gail Mitchell
R.A.F. Coningsby visitors centre in particular Mr. Jim Balsom
Mr. David Barnett local historian (Lancaster bomber crash)
Mr. David Wallis, Nancy and John Mileman, Grimsby & Cleethorpes philatelic society for currency research
Mrs. Margaret Powell for loan of coins
Mr.Rob Simons for loan of coins
The Watford observer newspaper in particular Michael Pickard, chief reporter
Marion Jones for printed article
Imperial war museum in particular David Bell and his team, researchers, licensing and photographic teams in particular Edgar Aromin, Mariusz Gasior, Yvonne Oliver, Pauline Allwright Josephine Garnier, Christopher Deal and Yolande
North Thoresby news in particular Rev. Bob Emm
Robert Opie collections
Watford central library in particular Sue Brandon
Mrs. Greville (photographers) for the copy of Sandringham road devastation photograph
Alpine press – Kings Langley
Comley cameras, Cleethorpes, in particular, Mark

(Imperial war museum images may not be reproduced without prior permission from the imperial war museum)

Dedications to school teachers and school friends

Mr. Judd junior school Headmaster
Miss Simpson
Miss Butler
Miss Badcock
Mr. Taylor
Mr. Tucker
Miss Clifford Headmistress of senior school
Mrs Burns
Miss Goodhall
Mrs Corcoran
Miss Moore
Miss Larratt
Miss Loveday
Miss Jackson
Miss Craven
Miss Hardwick

Mary Denham
Peggy Eyres
Geraldine Camm
Peter Curtis
Tony Sterling
Mary and John Fuller
Diana Reed
Margaret Williams
June Laidlaw
Nora Conroy

Joyce and Jean Eadie
Jean Towfield
Maureen Smith
Terence Meadows
Kenneth Plumb
Brian Timberlake
Barbara Teague
June Shears
Joan Blackhall
Mary Carter
Terry Meadows

My dearest friend Denise, without whom my war would have been very dull.

4

Introduction

A Different Kind of Childhood

This book is simply written for adults and children. The social history and the escapades of two little girls throughout the war years will bring laughter to the readers, and memories of days gone by to adults. It is a story creating good conversation when grandparents are asked "How was it When you Were Young?"

The era in which this story is written is definitely black and white. I have all the photographs and newspaper cuttings used in the story. Currency in those days was £.s.d. I have all the notes and coins together with a conversion table.

CHAPTER ONE
THE EARLY YEARS

Occasionally my mind is triggered off to memories of my childhood. Sometimes it is by newspaper articles or a television report, even a radio programme. I often say to myself, I used to do that or, I remember that or, perhaps, I went there. My life has not been over-indulged with money but it has been well fulfilled with love, laughter and exciting adventures.

This story is about me and my friend Denise. We have known each other for over seventy years. Our adventures throughout the Second World War will make you laugh and sometimes a tear will fall from your eyes.

I was born before the outbreak of the Second World War and lived with my parents in Surrey. They rented a house near my Father's work. He was a compositor in a printing factory. His job was to put together words made from individual metal letters which were placed in a shallow wooden tray. This would be placed in the printing machines, brushed with ink, which would transfer the words on to paper. This method was used by printers for all kinds of printed matter such as books and leaflets and information that needed to be communicated to other people.

His job was not well paid so he decided that he had to move us to a bigger town and get a job with a bigger company which would pay higher wages, so we moved to Watford in Hertfordshire in 1936.

A newly built house on an Avenue in a new estate was to be our home for the next thirty years. This was a very modern house. We had electric light, an Ascot water heater and a gas pipe. These three utilities transformed our lives. No longer did we have to bathe in a tin bath in front of the kitchen fire. We could heat the flat irons on the gas cooker to do the family ironing and, best of all, we could switch the electric light on by pressing a switch fixed to all the walls in the house doing away with the gas mantle.

This house was rented as the cost of buying such a property was far beyond our means. The rent man called each Friday to collect his money which was always in an envelope and placed on the bottom stair. We now lived in a three bedroom semi-detached house, this meant that I had my own bedroom, a small bedroom with a bed and dressing table at the front next to my parent's double bedroom.

Our new home 1937. I was four years old

My Mother and Father were very proud of their home. All the rooms had linoleum floor coverings with slip mats beside the beds. The staircase had a narrow carpet that ran the full length from the top landing to the front hall. There were brass stair-rods which were fitted into each stair tread keeping the carpet in place. Each side of the carpet was painted wood. No fitted carpets in those days.

Money was very short in our lives and moving to a new house was a great strain on resources. My Mother did not go out to work. Working women were frowned upon. A woman's place was in the home. Only the men went out to work. My Father used to walk two miles to work in the morning, four miles there and back at lunch time then two miles home for the evening. He had a promotion soon after we moved which meant he had to work permanently on night shift. This meant that we very rarely met. He was going to bed as I was going to school and he was getting up for work soon after I came home at the end of my school day.

Clothes at that time were very dull. Women made the best of themselves but as they didn't leave the house very often, certainly not socially, they made little effort to make themselves attractive. Here again, if they had tried to improve their clothes public opinion would have called them 'a hussy', which was not complimentary. In hindsight, I think I felt a kind of security in the knowledge that I knew what my Mother was likely to be wearing and it would all be covered up by a wrap over apron. I had a cosy, warm feeling inside me as I walked home from school knowing she would answer the doorbell. Whatever she did in the day-time, she was always there for me at home time.

A brown gabardine raincoat and a matching beret, brown court shoes and lisle stockings (which could be darned) was her everyday shopping outfit, never changing until the mid forties. If the weather was bad she would wrap a scarf around her neck and if it snowed, she wore gaiters to keep her feet and legs dry. These were made of brown leather, with a fleecy lining, buttoned up the side of the leg and an elastic strip that fitted under her shoe.

Sometimes she wore galoshes (a rubber overshoe) over her court shoes to keep her feet dry. She was a slightly built person, not very tall. Her hair was dark brown (she called it auburn) which she kept in the same style all her life (77 years), a parting on the right side, a wave on the left side and a roll of curl stretching from one ear around the back of her head to the other ear. She never wore make-up as her face had a natural rosy glow. She loved a joke (within the family) and very rarely showed her displeasure outside the home. She never smacked me but she would often take me to one side if she was cross with me and say "Little girls should be seen but not heard."

Advertising was in its infancy, women were not encouraged to buy the latest garments or to follow the latest fashion. Cinema was emerging from silent films in black and white. Colour photography and printing would change the way women thought about themselves in the future, but in these times shoes had to go to the repairers, socks had to be darned and clothes had to be mended.

Hair had to be cut on bath nights, which was usually on a Friday. If the weather was cold we would have a tin bath which would be half-filled with warm water in front of the coal fire in the dining room. In summer we would use the big bath in the new bathroom.

When we arrived at the house, the roads were still to be made up. The pavement areas were rough stones and I can remember the day the roads were tarred. I stood at the front gate and watched as the enormous steam roller with wheels of iron which towered above me, moved backwards and forwards over the wet tar. Dirty black smoke from the coal used to make the steam from the tall brass chimney stack on top of the roof of the driver's cabin. The workmen spread the tar by shovel over the shingle base. The noise was deafening and spasmodic as the steam roller moved back and forwards to press the tar flat.

An acrid smell arose from the hot asphalt which was choking. I couldn't stand watching all this for long as my eyes were watering. I ran indoors and watched from the front room window. My Mother ran around the house closing every window and putting a wet handkerchief over my nose and mouth to stop me breathing in the fumes. The whole day was frightening but also exciting, I had never seen anything like it before and I was happy to be safe indoors.

New paving slabs edged with roughened curb stones were being laid at the side of the tarmac creating a pavement over the rough shingle on which we had been walking. A further introduction brought added excitement as The Electricity Board were installing tall street lights in the paving. No more gas lights in the street, very modern!

Buses were the main mode of travel. Modern ones were all closed in to keep the passengers dry when it rained. The bus conductors were always men. The man would issue a ticket for the journey from his ticket board. You had various coloured tickets according to the price you paid for your journey. He would punch a hole in your ticket with his punching machine hanging from his neck when you handed him the fare for your journey.

I enjoyed collecting the coloured tickets that had been thrown on the floor of the bus to see how many colours I could collect. There was a way of folding the tickets on top of one another making a long concertina, just for fun. The trams were still running but most of them were open to the elements and were much slower than the buses. They didn't continue in service very long once the motor buses came into operation. The tram lines were removed from the roads and new surfaces were laid for the new modern motor cars.

Our new house was quite a distance from the nearest shop but once we arrived at the main road we were well served by the basic shops. The butcher, the oil/hardware shop, the paper shop where we bought our sweets, the grocers and greengrocers and a little further along the post-office. All were around half an hours walk from our house. The Doctor's surgery was quite a long way from home but as we had to pay to see the Doctor - we didn't call there very often.

My Grandma Thorburn (my Mother's Mother) would come to us occasionally for a few days holiday. She used to spend hours with me when she came to stay. I was always on her lap being read to or being taught to read. She had infinite patience and, as I was her grandchild, she was determined to give me as much education as she could. I could read and write well before I started school. I knew my alphabet forwards and backwards thanks to her.

The shops in the high street, about four miles away, were all illuminated. Now that electricity was available the shops were open until ten o'clock, the shop assistants used to work long hours. They were well trained, civil and polite to customers. The adage "The customer is always right" was taken very seriously. The shop assistants post was an important position in those days. They needed to be able to add up correctly and give the right change to customers. Drapery shops needed to have competent assistants that could measure and advise customers on correct lengths needed for making up clothes and curtains.

Paying for your purchases used to fascinate me. The sales assistant would write out the bill and ask for our money then she would put them both into a hand size barrel attached to a wire which was suspended from the ceiling. The wire would stretch from the counter to a small office away from the serving area. She would pull the handle and the little barrel would travel along the wire which led to the office. Here the bill was checked and any change that was due to the customer was put inside the barrel and sent whizzing down the wire back to the shop assistant who then unscrewed the barrel and gave the bill and change to the customer.

CHAPTER TWO
THE START OF THINGS TO COME

I followed my Mother everywhere until the day I went to school. As I was her only child, she was my playmate and my teacher. I learned gardening skills, knitting, sewing and embroidery, even cooking, especially at Christmas. I would stir the Christmas pudding mixture and count the silver three penny pieces (we called them joeys) as they were stirred in to the mixture, making sure that when the pudding was eaten we could account for the same number that went in as were on the side of our plate.

I can remember the first day at school very well. I had just had my fifth birthday in December and on the eighth of January 1938 I went to school. It was bitterly cold and I was wearing my new school coat, it was too big and too long for me. A big scarf was wrapped around my neck and shoulders. My Mother walked me along the road and through a short cut which was called the "alley". We passed a small bungalow which had been turned into a shop and was run by a formidable looking lady called Mrs. Miller, a short dumpy woman with grey hair that appeared to stick out from all over her head. On her feet she wore ill fitting slippers. She had Pekinese dogs running around her and a cigarette hung from her lips. My Mother impressed upon me that when I was big enough to walk to school on my own, I was to walk past the bungalow and on no account was I to go inside the shop.

This was the first time that I had walked along the "alley". We passed the bowling green on the left hand side. Further on there was a children's recreational playground. I was fascinated by the swings, see-saw, climbing frame and roundabout. I had a swing in the back garden but it was not as big as these. I would rather have played on the swings instead of going to school. My Mother promised me that she would take me into the playground after school when the days were longer but it was too cold and dark at four o'clock on a cold January afternoon.

We walked on to the school. As we turned into the playground, through big iron gates I began to wish we could go home. Hand in hand we entered the big school doorway, the children's cloakroom was on the left but we read the notice pinned to the door. All new children should walk into the school hall where they were to be registered. After registration I was taken out through the big doors through which we had come, to the small school. This was a low wooden building across the playground from the big school. My Mother followed on until we came to three concrete steps leading to the entrance door, at this point I was told to say good-bye to her. I shook with fear and wanted reassurance that she would be at the school gates to meet me at the end of the day to take me home. She gave me my lunch (two sandwiches in a paper bag) and turned for home, I dutifully went with this lady up the steps into the corridor.

My breath was taken away by a huge wooden rocking horse. It was sitting outside my new classroom. I wondered if I would ever be allowed to ride on it. The door opened and I was gently pushed in to the classroom to meet my teacher. Miss Simpson was a very tall lady with grey hair tied in a bun at the back of her neck. She was wearing a long smock over her clothes.

I was told to sit down, given a slate and slate pencil and told to draw whatever I liked and listen to Miss Simpson while she calmed down the tearful members of the class. She spoke very firmly to them. She put up with no nonsense and very soon there was quiet except for the screeching of slate pencils on slate boards. The rest of the day was taken up with our milk drink and opening our lunch bags. Then it was playtime in the playground if the weather was dry otherwise it was playing with board games in the classroom.

Eventually we were told to sit back at our tables and get ready for our story which I enjoyed. Then the hand-bell was rung and it was time to go home. We were taken to our pegs in the cloakroom, Miss Simpson was there to help us do up buttons and see us off the premises. It was time to go out in the cold and go home.

During the spring of 1939 a new girl joined the class. Her name was Denise Scott. She was a pretty little girl with ash blonde wavy hair. She wore a pinafore dress with a jumper and cardigan and knee length socks. Her Mother called her "Den" but she made it quite clear to me that her name was Denise'a but I could call her Denise! I shortened her name to Dennie when I grew to know her better.

My Mother knew Mrs. Scott and it was decided that I should walk to school with her and Denise. I was not too happy about this, but as I had now moved up to a higher class I felt older than Denise and as I knew she was going into Miss Simpson's baby class, I could cope with walking to school after all, I had left the baby class a month ago!

We forged a firm friendship which has lasted over seventy years. We've had our good and bad times but the bond between us has always enabled us to overcome our differences. We sometimes had childish arguments. I always came off worst at these times. I thought my world had come to an end then and I shed gallons of tears. It was so bad that my Mother had to walk me to school because I was afraid of Denise and her new friends attacking me or calling me bad names. It was always Mrs. Scott who offered to take me to the pictures with Denise if we made friends and behaved ourselves. I can remember the first film I saw was "Dumbo", a baby elephant with very large ears who was caught in a fire in a high rise building and when he was jumping off the top to save his life he found that his ears would help him to fly.

Another film was "Bambi", Bambi was a young deer whose Mother was caught by a woodland fire and he had to fend for himself while he was growing up. I cried quietly into my hankie, I quite forgot that I was with Mrs. Scott and not my Mother. After the film we went to the ice-cream shop to cheer ourselves up as Denise had been crying too.

My Mother was a great knitter and needlewoman. She kept both of us well dressed. One particular event sticks in my memory. I did so want to wear a new cardigan to school. It was canary yellow. She had spent hours knitting it and it was supposed to be kept for wearing on special occasions. She had also made me a Royal Stewart tartan kilt to go with it. I begged her to let me wear it all to school.

15

One bright sunny day off I went to school with Denise and I was wearing my new clothes. I must have been around six years old. During the lunch break, I met Denise and suggested that we go round the back of the school to look at the gardens and see if the bulbs had come through. I felt that I would impress Miss Simpson and she would be proud of me if I could tell her of the gardens progress.

I knew the gardens were out of bounds but I would frequently push out the boundaries. Not realizing that I was doing anything wrong, Denise followed me and, once again, I could not help looking under the school building. I saw a large 'Allie'. This was a marble that had rolled under the school from a game that had been played in the playground the other side. I thought that I would crawl under the school and retrieve it. Off I went, slowly at first. Nearing the 'Allie' I heard the school bell ringing,

Denise shouted, "I'm off to school"

With that she was gone. Realizing that I could not turn round in this tight space I crawled backwards, clutching my "prize". When I arrived at the edge of the building I was horrified to see two very large feet in black pointed shoes facing me. It was Miss Simpson. She hauled me out and gave me a hard smack. I was told to stand in the school hall for the rest of the morning.

My new bright yellow cardigan was now filthy dirty. My face was black and my hands and knees grazed, and I stood there worrying about my Mother's reaction when she saw me at the end of the day. When I arrived home and rung the door bell my Mother's face was like thunder and I was sent to my room.

The following week the workmen arrived to put wire netting around the base of the school.

CHAPTER THREE
CONFIDENCE

The first Christmas I can remember was when my Father took over the ownership of a car from his friend Sidney Rule who had joined the Auxiliary Air Force. He took my Father out for a few drives to get him used to the controls. In those days it was not necessary to pass a driving test. You could either drive or you couldn't.

He decided to drive us down to Portsmouth to spend Christmas Day with my Grandma Thorburn. There was no Christmas tree or decorations in poorer people's homes. It was a case of a glass of port or sherry and a slice of Christmas cake, a hug and kiss and off to see the next member of the family. The whole day was spent visiting aunts and uncles and then the long drive back home. My Father didn't drink. He was a tea-totaller. I met lots of aunts, uncles and cousins I didn't know I had.

After my sixth birthday Denise and I walked to school on our own. There were several children walking the same route, some were friendly, but some were not. We all walked through the alley passing a huge sycamore tree which was growing between the alley and a private garden. I was very worried about that tree, it seemed to be magical as the great branches spread themselves over the top of the alley. In winter it appeared black and I imagined that eyes were watching me from the bird holes pecked in it's trunk; that rats and mice would run up and down and bats would fly from it's top most branches and scream at me as they whirled round and round. As time passed my fears were compounded, not by my imagination but by physical bullying.

I suffered with ear ache a lot, especially in cold weather. My Mother knitted me a pixie hood in bright yellow wool with long straps that tied under my chin. It was lovely and warm in the cold weather, and helped to take the pain away from my ears. Some of the not so friendly children would creep up behind me and pull at the point of my hood as they passed me on the way to school. There were four or five of them. They were older than us, Denise and I called them the "nasty gang".

On one occasion when Denise was not with me, the nasty gang caught up with me as I walked alone on my way home from school. They tied me by my pixie hood straps around my neck on to the wire fencing behind the sycamore tree. I tried not to cry but I was very frightened and, as it was beginning to get dark, I thought I would have to stay there tied up all night. The nasty gang ran off laughing. I struggled to release the knot that tied me to the fence and managed to free myself. I walked home slowly and peeped around each corner to make sure that the "nasty gang" were not waiting for me, I was really terrified and the tears streamed down my cheeks. There was no one about to help me, and my neck was quite sore, I thought I would die before I arrived home.

That night when I was getting ready for bed my Mother noticed the red mark round my neck. I told her about the incident that happened that afternoon, and how frightened I was. She gave me a big hug and kissed my cheek. I knew she felt sorry for me, she promised to give me a treat when I had washed and dressed myself for bed. I had on a pink fluffy dressing gown and pink bed socks (I had a hot water bottle which would have burned my feet without my bed-socks). She lifted me up on to the window sill and sang to me,

> Twinkle, twinkle, little Star
> How I wonder what you are,
> Up above the world so high
> Like a diamond in the Sky.

I copied her and together we looked through my bedroom window, with the lights off, into the dark night sky, we sung the rhyme together, the stars twinkled and I felt that I was secure with my Mother's arms around me. I slept soundly that night.

I began to dread wearing the pixie hood but my Mother insisted on putting it on me every morning (she was knitting me another one in bright blue!). On another occasion I was walking on my own to school in the morning and I saw the "nasty gang" waiting for me at the start of the alley. I ran back home and knocked on the door telling my Mother that I was not feeling well. She laughed at me and walked me back to school. I never told her why I wasn't feeling well.

When I arrived at school I was late for registration and I was made to stand in the corridor until assembly was over. The "nasty gang" saw me and began to laugh. I became very anxious, I wanted to tell my teacher why I was late for school and what the "nasty gang" was doing to me but I was afraid of what they might do to me if I "split" on them.

I was going to have to find another route to get to and from school. I knew there was one, but it was a much longer walk on the pavement along the main road, which meant I needed to leave home earlier in the morning to get to school on time and I would arrive home later in the afternoon. After thinking a little about this idea I decided to stay as I was and bravely walk to and from school on my own. I hoped that it would not be long before Denise was better and able to come to school with me. She would know what to do to keep us safe.

When I told her what had been happening she thought that we should wait until a grown-up walked past the school gates and along to the alley and we could walk in front or behind them pretending that we knew them and then we could get passed the "nasty gang" that way. That was the way it was for a while. When the better weather came I did not need to wear my pixie hood because my earache had left me and I felt much better.

During the summer months we walked through the alley without any bother because the daylight helped us to see who or what was in front or behind us. As our confidence grew we felt more secure in the fact that an adult was not far away. Soon we began to forget the "nasty gang" and we walked on our own without an adult around. I don't know what happened to the "nasty gang", but they certainly didn't bother us any more.

Denise had her sixth birthday on February 14th. I went to tea with her. Parties were out as far as making a spread was concerned, but she did have a birthday cake. Her present from her parents was a fairy cycle. It was dark green with thick pump-up tyres. I spent a lot of time sitting on our front room window sill watching Mr. Scott running up and down the road holding on to the saddle while Denise pedalled away. She wobbled quite a bit at first but she soon got the hang of it. On the second day Mr. Scott let go of the saddle and Denise was off pedalling on her own – she could now ride a bicycle. I begged her to let me ride it but she kept it to herself. I envied her that bicycle.

She had an elder sister, Eileen and an older brother, Richard. Eileen was working in a munitions factory on war work making parts for guns and rifles. One day while she was leaning over her special machine, her hair became entangled in a wheel of the fast moving piece of equipment and caught her hair ripping a large area of her scalp away which kept her from work for several weeks. She spent a few days in hospital then several weeks at home recovering. After that incident all the munitions factory workers had to wear headscarves as turbans to keep their hair away from the machines. Of course, most factory workers were women on war work and their hair was very important to them.

After a few weeks of watching Denise ride her bicycle, I couldn't wait any longer to have a try at riding it myself. She asked her Father to help me learn to ride the bicycle. I had watched her learning, and it wasn't long before I too could ride that bicycle but it was many years before I owned one.

Our time in the small school was soon to end as we were both nearly seven years old. It was time to join the big school. On our last day we were given some "sweets" and played games and said our good-byes to our teachers. Miss Simpson gave us a hug and off we went with all the other seven year olds to the junior school.

We were introduced to a much different school day. The slates and pencils were no-where to be seen. Here we had paper writing books. Gone were the small tables we used to sit at, here we had desks with lift up lids and ink wells, some of us were allowed to write with pen and ink but most were using pencils.

Denise and I were able to be in the same class but we were not allowed to sit together. Our first junior school teacher was Miss Butler. She was a pretty lady with lovely blond wavy hair. Sometimes on games day, she would wear a gym slip and join in our games of rounders and a new game we were to learn, netball. This was played on the school playground and we were told that sometimes we would form a team and play a team from another school when we were older.

I enjoyed games. On one particular games afternoon, we were on the playing field learning about running races, I had been chosen to try for the Town school sports day, I lined up with the other class members but I never heard the start whistle, every one had run off and I was left standing. Miss Butler shouted at me

"Wake-up Jean don't just stand there, run".

I didn't like her much after that. All was forgiven when I was selected to run in the Town sports day representing our junior school although I was not placed in the first three, I was proud to know that I had been chosen to represent our school.

We were coming to the end of the long summer school holiday when the outbreak of the Second World War began. I remember the pictures in the paper of Mr. Neville Chamberlain returning from his visit to Germany in 1938. He was holding the famous telegram in his hand which he had received from Adolf Hitler, the leader of the German people, assuring the British People there would be "peace in our time". There would be no war.

On the 3rd of September 1939, I was outside Woolworths store in North Watford with my Mother. A van with a tan-noy system attached to the roof, drove slowly along the road, relaying the message that war had been declared at 11 a.m. on the morning of the 3rd September 1939. We could not believe it. What had happened to that promise to Mr. Chamberlain that there would be no war? My Mother gripped my hand tightly as we walked very quickly back home to await more news on the wireless.

My first school photograph 1939

On the way we passed Mr. Blackburn's shoe repair shop. He had a special piece of equipment that re-charged accumulator batteries. These batteries consisted of a square glass jar about the size of a milk bottle with a black carrying handle around the neck. They were filled with an acid liquid. There was a connection device on the lid which when this was standing at the back of the wireless the leads were connected to a lead from the wireless which completed the electrical circuit to make our wireless operate. There were very few radios in those days. We collected one battery to make sure we had enough charge in our wireless to listen to the news and to follow the instructions that were to be given to everyone.

No-one was panicking but there was an air of concern about the place. People were confused. We couldn't believe we were at war. Bicycle bells were ringing as their riders were in a hurry, buses were full of passengers in the middle of the morning. The first thing we did when we arrived home was to put the kettle on, find a piece of paper with a pencil and, as we sipped our hot tea, we put the wireless on, ready to take down any messages. We listened to Alva Liddell, the newscaster, who gave us our instructions which the Government had worked out for everyone in the country.

We were all to have gas masks. This was to be carried at all times, no matter where we were or whatever we were doing. They would be supplied complete with a brown cardboard box and notes of instruction. We had to collect them from a designated shop in our area. They had to be signed for to make sure everyone had one. There were special ones for babies, they were very large and acted as a cradle. The baby was put inside and then it was sealed so that any gas released in the air could not harm the baby.

When we collected ours we had to try them on and all three of us sat round the kitchen table with the masks on our faces. We did laugh but as we laughed our warm breath steamed up the small viewing window and as for the brown box, one shower of rain would help it to disintegrate and the cord to go around our necks would soon pull through the holes in the box. When we had stopped laughing we realized that these masks could save our lives and they were to be treated with respect and we would do as we were told and carry them everywhere.

All homes, factories and offices had to install black-out curtains or boards to cover the windows. This was to protect the communities from overhead enemy aeroplanes. Any lights on the ground would help the enemy aeroplanes to find out where they were when flying at night. My Mother made black curtains which hung at the windows all around the house. It became a ritual every day to close the curtains at dusk and open them in the morning. All the street lights were disconnected and shop signs were turned off. This was not too bad in the summer but dreadfully dangerous in the winter.

Warden with gas mask, we were all issued with a mask.
Imperial War Museum N.D.3494

We had to protect our windows by sticking brown sticky paper strips from corner to corner on all our windows to stop cracking or breaking glass falling from bomb blast. Incendiary bombs were the next problem. They were dropped by enemy aeroplanes.

My Mother kept two galvanized buckets on the landing, one for water and one for sand, also a step ladder leaning against the spare room door to enable her to get through the trap door into the loft if a bomb came through.

We were on our own at night time because my Father worked on the night shift. Fortunately no bombs came through our roof but it was sensible to take precautions. We did lose some roof tiles due to a bomb falling near-by but that was all the damage we incurred during the whole of the war.

Life went on very much as normal, Denise and I walked to school in the usual way. One Monday morning we arrived at the school gates to find a huge, thick, brick wall had been built during the weekend in front of the main school glass doors. Enough room had been left for children to walk into school but not enough room to ride a bicycle between the wall and the doors.

We were told at assembly that morning that the wall had been built to stop the blast from any exploding bombs affecting the school entrance.

Our junior school with the bomb blast protection wall 1939.
Image courtesy of Watford Museum

CHAPTER FOUR
DARK HORIZONS

My Father brought a new magazine home from his printing factory. It was called "Picturegoer" and was full of film star pictures and stories about famous people. I liked this magazine. My favourite film stars were Sonja Heanie. She was a world champion ice skating star but she also acted in films. My other favourite famous film star at that time was Esther Williams, she was a world champion swimmer.

I used to take my precious magazine to school to show my friends. I felt very important when at break time they all stood around me looking at the magazine. Some of them wrote to the film stars asking for their pictures, I didn't have enough money to pay the postage to send to America to get some pictures for myself. When they received them they were also signed by the stars.

One day I would learn to swim, but I knew I would never be as good as Esther Williams but that would not be until the war was over because all our swimming pools were now closed. Most of the beaches around our Island were covered in barbed wire and barricades to stop the enemy landing from the sea.

Large air raid shelters were erected in the streets. The war had not affected every-day life yet! But the government assured the people that shelters were to be built and that they could take refuge in them when the bombs came to our country. All homes had the opportunity to have their own air raid Anderson shelters in their gardens or the choice of a Morrison indoor shelter which would take up half the living space in one room.

My parents decided to have their shelter in the garden. Our neighbours helped each other to dig a 6 x 6 and 4 foot deep hole in the ground to erect their "Anderson" shelter. There were two bunk bed supports in each shelter. Denise and I watched with interest and glee when the shelter had been erected – another place to play.

The wails of the warning siren warbled up and down, the very sound of them filled you with fear. They were dreadful but the all-clear was a one note wail which continued for a few minutes to let you know it was safe to carry on life as normal. We hoped that we would never have to listen to these sirens but it was still early days in this war.

Our air raid shelter was similar to this one.
Imperial War museum N.HU54730

18½s Register To-day

Men of 18½—those born between January 1 and June 30, 1923—register to-day for service with the Forces. They are the first class to register since the Government announced the new Conscription plans.

Although they are the youngest group to register and it is expected they will be called up within the next month, they will not be required to serve abroad until they are 19. Men wanting to join the Air Force or Navy were given an opportunity to do so.

Men over 18 were being called-up to join the Army, Navy and Air Force. At first the selection was by age. My Father was not in the younger age group and we hoped that he would not be affected. He continued to work at night. My Mother did her gardening and I went to school, but somehow we were all uneasy. We realized that if the air raid siren went off we could all be in different shelters at the same time and not able to look after each other. Children began to learn self reliance very early in their lives. The daily news on the wireless was telling us of frightening events and happenings in other countries.

My parents made a quick decision to visit both sets of their parents before the war engulfed us all. We travelled by train to London and then on to Portsmouth. Grandma Thorburn and two aunts and their families lived close to each other. Families used to live within calling distance of each other in those days. There were no cars and all visiting had to be done on foot.

My Grandma was a Scotswoman and would insist on calling me 'Bairn'. We arrived at her home. There was no front garden. We passed from the pavement, through the front door and down one step into the sitting room. On the right hand side was a cabinet which housed a gramophone on top of which stood a beautiful statue of a boy with his arm above his head and he was holding a cherry above his mouth. I wanted to touch him but my Mother whispered in my ear

"Keep your hands to yourself and don't touch a thing".

I heeded her warning but my eyes were everywhere. We walked through to the parlour straight from the sitting room, there was no hallway. It was nice and warm and very cosy. There was a black cooking range on one side of the room with a big black kettle hissing away on top of the range. At that moment we heard a hand bell ringing outside and my Grandma opened the door of a huge kitchen cupboard and told me to get a jug of milk from the milkman. She opened the front door and to my amazement, I looked out on to a gaily painted cart with a horse in harness and the milkman holding out his ladle. I gave him my halfpenny and jug which he filled from the milk churn which was in the cart and I returned indoors to my Grandma.

There was a lovely gas lamp hanging from the ceiling with a little chain hanging from it. If you wanted to light the lamp you pulled the chain and the lamp would come down to enable you to hold a lighted taper to the lamp. When the lamp lit you would pull the chain and the lamp would rise back towards the ceiling or to make the light stay in any position you needed, to give you the best light for whatever you were doing.

The kitchen was called the scullery where the washing-up was done in a stone sink, it was quite large but very shallow and just one tap, cold water only. In the corner was a washing boiler, this was heated by gas which you lit on wash days and bath days. There was a long tin bath hanging from a nail on the outside wall of the kitchen, it was brought indoors on bath nights and put on the floor in front of the kitchen range. I was amused to find that I had to walk down the yard (not the garden) to a little brick built building, inside there was a toilet seat perched over a hole in the ground, the door was a wooden one with a wide gap both top and bottom. My Mother followed me with a bucket of water to swill away whatever I needed to do in the toilet!

In the far corner of the parlour was a wooden door built into the wall behind which was a spiral staircase. At the top of the stairs there were two doors, a door to the left and one to the right which opened on to the two bedrooms. My Grandma had brought up six children on her own in this small house. Her husband had been in the navy and had been lost at sea during the First World War when a ferocious storm hit his ship and it floundered and sank, drowning all officers and crew. Before we left she gave me a gift of a junior wash tub, scrub board and brush to wash my dolls clothes. I was thrilled with this and couldn't wait to get home. (It all fitted into a shoe box!)

On the way back home we had to travel through London. My parents decided that we should visit my Father's parents before going home. They lived in Finsbury Park. Their living accommodation was very different. This part of London was built for the well off

Victorian families who would have had servants but in the late 1930s these large properties had begun to change into multi family homes and this is what had happened to my Grandparents. The house they lived in consisted of four storeys above ground and one apartment below ground level.

Grandma Thorburn. No. 1 Cross Street Southsea 1939

We had to climb up one flight of stairs that led from the pavement to the front door to visit them. There was another flight of steps that led down to the basement apartment. The door was always open in the day-time but closed at night. There was one family living below my Grandparents and two families above all sharing one staircase. The kitchen was very small and lit by gas lighting. It had a small black kitchen range and a large stone sink with one tap.

From the kitchen there were three steps down to a small landing and three steps up to get to the sitting room and the bedroom. The sitting room was at the front of the house but it was dark and dismal, the curtains were never drawn apart because the sunlight would fade the furniture. Across the sitting room was a sideboard which was very long and ornate. On this stood a gramophone which had a huge brass trumpet on the top and on a side table was a very large green plant, I was told that it was an aspidistra!

We walked back to the kitchen and waited for the tea to be made, I was bored and sidled out of the kitchen and found it great fun jumping across the three steps up to the second three steps. My Grandma stopped me. She said I would disturb the people in the flat below and I was to sit quietly and read a book. She was a very large lady, wrapped in a large pinafore, wearing earphones on her head because she was very deaf. She would sit me on her knee, I hated this. Her chest would go in and out with her heavy breathing and the perspiration caused by any exertion, would stand out on her brow.

She probably loved me very much as I was her only grandchild. My Father was her only child, but I'm pleased we didn't visit very often. Soon it was time to say our farewells. She gave me a doll to take home, it was a very ugly doll, probably the very latest design in dolls, it was all double jointed, very long with dark curly hair. I called it Clara. My Grandparents hugged and kissed me and I struggled to get away. With tears running down her cheeks she kissed my Father good-bye. She knew how savage war could be. She had lived through the First World War, and now we were approaching another World War. None of us knew if we would see each other again.

This was the longest period of time I had ever spent with my Father. He never spent much time with me. He never read to me or played games or sat me on his knee. On this day it was shared with so many other people, I felt quite overpowered by meeting and talking to so many relations. I felt so safe with my parents. Dreaming

31

of my doll's wash board and wash tub, I fell asleep on the train from London and my Father carried me most of the way home.

CHAPTER FIVE
THE BEGINNING OF WAR

On 3rd of September 1939 war was declared between Great Britain and Germany. The Germans invaded Poland and were marching through Europe, killing and smashing everything that stood in their way. Their aim was to conquer the whole of Europe which would create the German Empire. Fortunately, as we are an Island, we had the safety of the English Channel between France and ourselves. Early on in the war they did invade and capture the Channel Islands, but we on the mainland felt safe from invasion.

In 1940 our everyday lives changed with the arrival of the ration book! Every man, woman and child had their own ration book. It was made up of sheets of small date printed coupons which would provide them with enough, though meagre, food to exist on without extras for three months. We would rather have lost our bank books than our ration books.

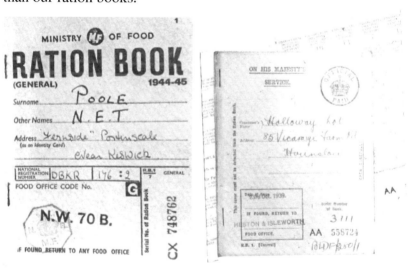

Ration Book   Meat Coupons
(By Kind Permission of Robert Opie Collections)

The ration book was a convenient size to fit into a handbag. It had a beige cover with black lettering. It was divided between groceries/toiletries and meat. Tinned foods were on a points system. The allowances for an adult were more than those for a child. My Mother had two and a half ration books which could be added together when shopping. The allowances could be saved up but the coupons could only be used once. Every item bought had to be paid for and the coupon in the ration book had to be cancelled by the grocer either by penning a line through the allowance square or to cut the square out with scissors. Shopping expeditions took far longer and the queues were stretching well outside the shop doors. No-one seemed to get upset about this. There was no more, "Popping to the shops," it was more "I've put a casserole in the oven it should be done by the time I get home!"

In 1944 the weekly allowance for one person:

4oz (100g)	Bacon or ham or a pork shop or 4 sausages
2oz (50g)	Cheese
4oz (100g)	Margarine
2oz (50g)	Butter
3pints (1800ml)	Milk, sometimes this allowance was dropped to 2 pints
8oz (225g)	Sugar
1lb (450g)	Jam every two months
2oz (50g)	Tea
Eggs	1 fresh egg a week sometimes 1 every two weeks
3oz (75g)	Sweet a week (we saved out ration up for four weeks so that we could get a choice at the shop)

Clothes were very limited. Fashion vanished from our lives and those items we could buy were bought with clothing coupons which were in a separate ration book with a red cover. Here again coupons had to be cancelled in the clothing coupon book. Sweets had their own set of coupons. Often people exchanged sweet coupons with one another for other things they preferred. Going to the sweet shop became an exciting adventure. Our monthly allowance gave us great problems in choosing from the array of sweets that were set before us. A small white paper bag held our ration for the month!

The Ration Books were provided by the Ministry of Food. To get one it was necessary to produce your Identity Card or Birth Certificate. There were no computers in those days so every entry was made by hand – everything took time but there was no use moaning, if you couldn't wait in a queue for your Ration Book you didn't eat, it was as simple as that. The food allowances were so meagre, for example, an adult was allowed 2ozs of cheese a week and a child 1oz. Small portions were the same for all groceries.

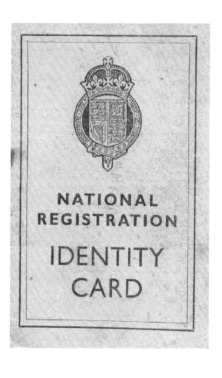

USE UP YOUR POINTS

"Herald" Food Reporter

THIS will be a beef-lamb week-end, with supplies of each evenly divided.

Cooked meat counters should have some pork luncheon meats and Canadian ham loaf.

In some shops there are plenty of small Camembert cheeses or Danish gorgonzola.

The domestic cheese ration will be reduced from 3oz. to 2oz. a week from Sunday.

FISH—rural areas are now getting better supplies; ORANGES—first of the new South African oranges will reach South Coast shops next week; APPLES—for London and the South and South-West, expected to arrive over the week-end go to those areas which had no share of Canadians.

But NEW POTATOES will generally be later this year.

Remember to clear up your points this week-end.

New ration book distribution starts on Monday.

Bread and flour were not rationed until later, but when that happened bread units were issued, more coupons to keep in your ration book. My Mother's favourite loaves were Farmhouse and Bloomer I liked the Cob because it had a crispy crust. I look at these portions when I measure out for my cooking now and wonder how on earth my Mother managed, especially when my Father went into the Army. She had to manage on one and a half rations!

Sweet coupons were fiercely guarded in our handbags. Our sweet rations were very meagre, two ounces a week for a child and the same allowance for adults. Cigarettes were not rationed and they were very cheap. They could be bought in packets of five, ten or twenty. They became the necessary nerve calming scourge of the country. Most adults had a packet of cigarettes in their pocket, it seemed that it was the only pleasure adults had. My Father smoked quite heavily, I hated his breath, tobacco turned his teeth black and stained his fingers yellow where he held his cigarette between them, he also had a chesty cough through smoking. I used to watch him as he disappeared in a cloud of blue smoke at meal times. I would ask to be excused from the table and run outside into the fresh air.

The Ministry of Agriculture and Fisheries organized a "Dig for Victory" campaign to get everyone digging in their gardens to grow their own food. It didn't take long for my Mother to start digging up her flower beds and plant potatoes and runner beans, she was very good at it. Harvest time was great, nothing nicer than walking down the garden with a basket and picking a handful of runner beans and a forkful of new potatoes. Cabbages were not quite as successful, the caterpillars got there first.

Another campaign was "Make do and Mend". All items of clothing had to be bought with enough coupons for the particular item you wanted to buy. Children were particularly heavy on shoes and socks. A lot of Brides had their wedding dresses and trousseau garments made from parachute silk. When parachutes had been used by the armed forces some of them could not be re-used, they were handed to brides to be, during the war.

The government had issued instructions to the Church Ministry that no Church Bells were to be rung for private occasions. They were to be rung continuously in the event of a German Invasion, it was deemed to be the quickest way of warning the people that they were in danger of being invaded and to give them time to make arrangements for their families. Fortunately this did not happen

My Mother would make my school blouses and nightdresses from old sheets. Summer dresses from her old ones. She kept me very well clothed. Hems were not allowed on clothes, neither were pleats, they took up too much material. The Make-do-and-Mend campaign came up with lots of ideas and articles were printed in newspapers. How to make a new dress from two old ones and then an apron from the pieces left over! Woollen jumpers were to be unravelled and re-knitted with different patterns. Odd balls of wool were used to make stripes in a new jumper.

The newspapers were also affected by lack of paper. The number of sheets in a newspaper were reduced. A few years into the war the one page newspaper appeared, at the worst time the newspapers were one sheet folded into four, but it told us all we wanted to know. No one moaned. We all understood the reason.

Furniture was a difficult item to buy. It was necessary to go to the Employment Office to explain why we needed an extra bed or a couple of chairs. We would be issued with a docket of agreement that we could buy the required item. All furniture was stamped with a Utility mark. Household linens were stamped to show that the fibres were of mixed origin. Cotton material bought by the yard was of a cheaper fibre than pure linen. Wood was from an inferior timber making the items more acceptable to the war effort.

A Utility mark

Imperial War Museum
HU 59828

Everything we needed to make life better had to be on ration – the whole country was on a 'save' footing. The ships that brought our food across the seas were being attacked and sunk by the German Navy. Submarines and U-boats were torpedoing our merchant vessels, thousands of merchant seamen lost their lives trying to bring food across the waters.

National Savings was encouraged by the Government throughout the country. Saving Certificates could be bought at various levels, seven shillings and six pence were the cheapest. There was one at fifteen shillings. The Government promised a good rate of return providing we could hold on to them for five or seven years. My Grandma Hunt bought me a fifteen shilling certificate on every birthday. I did not appreciate her good intentions as fifteen shillings pocket money would have been more acceptable at the time!

School children were encouraged to save by buying sixpenny saving stamps, they were stuck in a little book and when the book was full you could exchange the book for cash at the Post Office or have it transferred into your bank book. We could buy the stamps from our school teacher every Friday.

Another precaution the Government took to protect us all was to make it difficult for foreigners to find their way around our towns and villages. They were aware that the enemy paratroopers might be dropped from enemy planes during the hours of darkness. All our street names and signposts were removed. Anyone asking directions from local people were viewed with suspicion. There was a slogan for these times 'Careless Talk Costs Lives".

The Home Guard was formed. They were well informed, basically trained groups of ordinary men who learned how to use a rifle and what to do in an emergency. My Father had joined the local section of the Home Guard and he wore an army uniform. Another group called Air Raid Wardens was formed to walk round the streets after the light had faded. Often they would knock on peoples' doors if they could see any lights in their home which should have been protected by black-out curtains. They would shout through the letterbox: 'Put that light out'.

Home Guard, a civilian fighting force
Imperial War Museum N.H30442

Transport was another problem giving away our positions. Trains had blinds that pulled down over the windows and buses had to have their windows painted green to stop the light filtering through the windows.

Another group called Firewatchers were men whose duty it was to climb to the highest point in the area usually a Church tower, to watch for fires caused by falling bombs and to alert the fire engines to get to the fire as quickly as possible.

As the end of 1940 drew nearer the German aeroplanes began to bomb our country. London was their main target. Night after night, and during the day, the sirens wailed across the land and the drone of German aircraft could be heard. Thud, thud as the bombs fell and the guns fired and if it was a bright moonlit night we could expect wave after wave of enemy aircraft overhead. We felt quite safe in the day-time because not so many raids took place then and we also knew that my Father was asleep in bed and he would look after us. But at night-time it was different. We were on our own. When the siren went we used to stay up and sit by the fire. Sometimes we would make toast with the toasting fork held against the red embers of the fire. Marmite was our favourite spread on the toast. As tea was on ration we would drink hot fruit juice. When we heard the all-clear we would go off to bed.

I was nearing my eighth birthday when my earache came back with a vengeance. I was taken to the Doctor who told my Mother that I had an abscess in my ear and it needed urgent attention. The nearest hospital was a converted Asylum commandeered by the armed services to treat wounded soldiers from the battlefields. We took the bus to the hospital.

I remember walking along the road and looking at several square ambulances, painted green and brown with a big red cross on a white circle on the side. They were parked alongside one another in the car park. When we arrived, after walking down a long drive with dark overhanging trees, we were met by a uniformed soldier asking us the nature of our visit. He showed us to the entrance we needed.

The nurses were very kind to me. I left the hospital with bandages over my head and my pixie hood tied under my chin. The next day I went to school with my pixie hood back on my head and I sat in my classroom all day! It was several days before I was able to go outside to play but it was good not to have the earache.

The air raids became heavier, night after night the bombs fell and, again, it was mostly London that caught the brunt of the action. Night after night the sirens sounded and we sat downstairs drinking cups of tea. Sometimes I would put my fingers in my ears so as not to hear the bangs, but I worried that I would not hear something above us so I took my fingers out and sat quietly and waited. It was the waiting for something to happen that was the worst part as we sat together listening and wondering if my Father was safe as he was still working on night shifts. We used to worry about him working in that big factory and whether he would be safe walking home for his supper. At the same time he would be worrying about us alone in the house. We would wait for the all clear siren and creep up to bed. Sometimes I would creep into bed with my Mother because my bed was cold to go back to.

In 1942 the Government had approved a scheme to make school dinners available to all children of school age. This was mainly due to Mothers having to go off to war work and Fathers enlisting in the armed services. Although my parents were still at home, the idea of me getting a balanced meal in the middle of the day appealed to my Mother. The rations would go further so my name was put on the list for school meals.

The class teacher would call the school register on Monday morning along with the dinner register. She asked for the dinner money which was 1/- (one shilling) per day, 5/- for the week. Denise was the dinner monitor whose job it was to collect all the dinner monies from all the classrooms, take it up to the Headmaster's room and count it out. She had to balance the amount collected with the number of dinners required. She did this so well that the Headmaster told her she could come and work for him when she left school! Some children had free meals for various reasons. We never asked them why. We just accepted that that was the normal situation.

At lunch time we sat at tables of eight. We ate everything that was put in front of us because two teachers were walking up and down watching us. If we didn't clear our plates we were sent to the Headmaster's room and waited for his lecture on the reasons why we should eat our food, and how our Mothers tried hard to manage with shortages. Not many of us went in that direction because we were genuinely hungry. There were table monitors who cleared away the tables and chairs after we had eaten before the afternoon lessons could begin. We didn't mind doing that job because we could stay in the warm in the winter instead of going out into the playground.

One of the dinner monitors jobs was to set the teacher's table. This room was up a flight of stairs next to the Headmaster's room. I was on duty on one occasion when I had to carry a large bowl of runny custard with both hands up a flight of stairs without holding on to the banister rail, I learned a lesson in deportment that day.

Although we were a mixed school the girls and boys found their own games to play. Boys were always dashing about playing cowboys and Indians or cops and robbers and borrowing the girls skipping ropes to tie up their 'baddies'. The girls played with hoops and skipping ropes. Marbles involved both groups. The boys would always win. Whip and top was another playground activity. Some children were very good at this and had the top spinning all round the playground. There was always a teacher on duty patrolling the area keeping an eye on the children.

On Mondays most Mothers did their weekly washing and didn't bother about a mid-day meal for themselves but when we arrived back from school in the afternoons it was a doorstep of bread, without butter, but with jam. And if we were lucky, bubble and squeak for our hot tea. This was fried left-overs from Sunday lunch, with mashed potatoes, all nice brown and crispy which you could have with chutney or brown sauce. It was delicious.

CHAPTER SIX
A BIG CHANGE

When the national call-up began, all able bodied men between 18 and 25 joined one of the armed services, either, the Royal Navy, the Army or the Royal Air Force. Men over call-up age were detailed to enlist in the Home Guard.

I remember quite clearly my Father dressed in his home guard uniform walking in for his supper in between his duty shifts and, on one occasion, he brought his rifle home with him. He was very proud of his Royal Enfield, the same rifle that was being used on the battlefields of Europe! He stood it up in the corner and put an armchair in front of it just in case I became too inquisitive.

There had been a mass evacuation from all the schools in the London area. Parents were encouraged to send their children into the countryside away from the bombing before it started. Arrangements were made between schools in London and the War Ministry that all the children from each school should travel together. Parents were advised not to go on the platforms. All the good-byes were supposed to be said on the main concourse of the station but the instructions were all forgotten as the Mothers clung to their children until the last possible minute before the train pulled out.

Each child had a label tied to their blazers, a brown cardboard box which held their gas mask, and a small brown suitcase for their clothes. In each suitcase there was a stamped addressed envelope so that the children could write home and let their parents know where they were staying. The Government had agreed to send some children to Australia and Canada for safety. One of my Father's cousins went to Australia and was never heard of again. Sadly some children would never see their parents again because many of the parents were among thousands of citizens killed in the air raids. I was very lucky, I stayed with my parents.

The heavy bombing of London, known as "The Blitz" began in 1940 and went on for many months. Wave after wave of German aircraft let their bombs fall all over London. The King and Queen had two bombs on Buckingham Palace. They lived in the Palace all through the war years. They would visit areas that had been heavily bombed and talk to the people who were bombed out and no longer had homes to live in. They were fighting the war at ground level. They understood what it was like to have their homes bombed.

Whole communities were being moved away from London to the safety of the countryside. Barricades were erected around the Ministerial buildings in Whitehall, also national monuments were shrouded in timber to protect them.

I was suffering from tonsilitis and the doctor was called. He suggested that I had my tonsils and adenoids removed otherwise I was always going to have throat trouble, so it was decided that I should have the operation. I can remember my Mother asking him for his account and she paid him there and then. No NHS in those days! She had taken a war effort job in a local hospital. It was a private sanitorium but when all the hospitals in London were evacuated the London University College Hospital moved into the sanitorium.

As the men in the country were slowly joining the armed forces the women left at home were given the opportunity to work. The choices were munitions, hospitals or land Army, my Mother chose hospital work. The day arrived for my operation. I was able to have this carried out at the hospital where she worked. This meant that she didn't have to have time off work to nurse me and she could also visit me during the day whilst doing her war work. I can remember being wheeled on a trolley to the operating theatre and being told to count up to ten. Whether I ever arrived at ten I'll never know, but I do remember recovering from the operation and seeing my Father standing in the doorway in his Home Guard uniform holding my precious doll Sylvia. She was a very impressive doll, I think she must have been a wool shop model that sat in the window dressed in all kinds of beautifully knitted baby garments. I do know that I was only allowed to play with her on a Sunday afternoon whilst my Mother went to sleep in the armchair. I can also remember having a bowl of lovely cold ice cream to eat to soothe my very sore throat.

September 1941, it was a Saturday morning, the three of us were having our morning break drink in the garden and the doorbell rang. My Father went to answer the door and came back grinning all over his face holding a brown envelope in his hand, his call-up papers. I remember him saying, "Look out Jerry, I'm coming to get you".

My Mother didn't think it at all funny as she mopped her eyes and ran indoors, followed by my Father. I could hear raised voices from the kitchen,

"How could you be so excited Bert, you are leaving Jean and me alone whilst you go off to the war."

"I know it must seem like that to you, but so many of my mates have already gone and I seem to be the only one left and I want to go to do my bit," he replied.

I sat in the garden thinking about what I was going to do now that I was losing my Father. Would he be gone for long? Where would he have to go to and would he be safe? When would he come home?

After a little while we had a family discussion around the kitchen table. Both my parents were smoking cigarettes. (I had never seen my Mother smoke before.) Now we realized that there really was a war. My Mother decided that she could do with some shopping and I was sent off with a list. I was bemused. Was my Father really going to fight in the war? I dutifully went to the shops leaving my parents to sort out their dilemma.

October 1941 my Father reported for his training and donned his battledress at Catterick Camp. He joined The Royal Army Service Corps which served the troops by driving 3 ton vehicles, towing guns and anything that needed moving by land Although he joined as a driver, he had never passed a driving test (it wasn't necessary in those days). He did some training on heavy vehicles and was then transferred to Devises in Wiltshire. This was known as an in-transit camp where troops were sent before going overseas.

45

His letters arrived frequently and, with my help, my Mother soon learned how to read. She knew that she would have to concentrate on her writing because it was the only way she could keep in contact with my Father. I never realized that she had difficulty in reading and writing until this time. I had often wondered why she never read stories to me at bed-time when I was very small. We would have reading and writing lessons in the evenings now that my Father no longer came home for his supper break from work.

On the evening of my ninth birthday the doorbell rang and on the doorstep stood my Father. He had embarkation leave before going overseas. He had travelled by train to say good-bye to us before going off to join his unit. He knew nothing about where he was being sent. Those details were all very secret. No-one knew where their husbands and Fathers were. He promised to let us know as soon as he could.

My Mother decided that we should go to London to see him before he boarded the train for Southampton. He would need to change trains from Wiltshire in London and then from Waterloo station on to Southampton. For us it was easy to get to Waterloo. She decided to buy a new coat but she realized that she didn't have enough clothing coupons left so we made a quick visit to my Grandma Hunt in Finsbury Park to ask her for a few coupons. We walked the whole length of Seven Sisters Road in Finsbury Park looking into shop windows to find a suitable coat. This was not easy because all plate glass windows were boarded up against bomb blast damage. All we could do was to gaze through a small square window which was left unboarded. Eventually she found the coat she liked. She did look nice in it and we were off to the station with not much time to spare.

We saw my Father as he boarded the train for Southampton, I doubt whether he noticed her new coat she was wearing. After hugs and kisses along with all the other wives and families, we waved our farewells as the train pulled away from the platform. We stood with thousands of other women and a few children with a feeling of despondency, wondering what the future had in store for us all. How many of our men would not return. Would we survive the next few years? How long would it be before we met again? That day we were all doing the same thing, waving our men-folk off to war.

It was a quiet journey home on the train. In those days it was a steam train and my Mother repeatedly told me to keep away from the windows because they were black from the soot of the engine. It was still daylight and I enjoyed looking out of the carriage windows. I can remember the feeling of responsibility that came into my mind during that journey. One thing was for sure, I was going get on with the reading and writing lessons and the sooner the better otherwise my Father would not receive letters from her keeping him in touch with what was going on at home. I must admit that I had been shocked to find out that she had this difficulty. I knew she could write her name because I had seen her do it.

We were completely on our own now, and somehow we had to get through these days while we waited for my Father's return home after beating "Jerry". Some five and a half years later he returned to a very different world, wife and daughter. My Christian picture which hung on my bedroom wall now had a little verse written under it:

> Gentle Jesus meek and mild
> Look upon this little child,
> If I should die before I wake
> Gentle Jesus my soul to take
> Please bring my Daddy back home from the war.

CHAPTER SEVEN
A LATCH KEY KID

When Denise and I walked to school on a frosty morning we would pull up a weed from the hedgerows which had a long strong stem, strip the remaining leaves from it and bend the stem into a horseshoe and use it to collect all the glistening spiders' webs from the hedges. We scooped as many as we could gather running in front of each other to gain the best and biggest cobweb in a short time because we would have been late for school. Sometimes the loop would have still been full when we reached the school gates then we had to throw it away in the dustbin before going into the classroom.

I was allowed to have a door key of my own to enable me to let myself into the house when I returned from school in the afternoon. My Mother had to work until 6 o'clock each afternoon because the war work restrictions had been altered. To enable her to remain at the hospital she had to work a complete shift of at least six hours a day, twelve o'clock until six o'clock were her new hours.

I didn't mind in the summer because it was light until late in the evening and the days were warmer. The winter months were different. I hated coming home at 4 o'clock in the afternoon to a cold house and the darkness. Some days Denise and I would go into the kitchen and make ourselves bread and jam. No butter, that was precious and only saved for Sunday tea. Sometimes Mrs. Scott allowed me to sit and wait for Denise to have her tea, at least I was in the warm! Those days were hard to cope with especially if I had had a bad day at school. It seemed such a long wait to tell my Mother about my problems.

Occasionally we would lift down the jar of Cod Liver Oil of Malt (like runny toffee) from the top of the kitchen cupboard and eat it by the spoonful. This was supposed to give children extra vitamins in the winter months to keep colds away. Sometimes we would go to Denise's home and hide in the larder where Mrs. Scott kept her big stone jars of pickled onions. We would put our hands in the neck of the jar and pull out a few onions, they were delicious. We didn't take too many because we thought that she would notice that we had been to the jars (we didn't realize that she would smell the vinegar!).

Mr. Scott did not go into the war because he was a lot older than my Father which made him exempt from call-up. He continued to work each day as a printer and at night he was a fire watcher. He took up the call for "Dig For Victory" and grew his own vegetables for his family. He also had an allotment. It was in Garston Park, quite a walk from his home. He built himself a very large wheelbarrow to carry all the tools he wanted to use when he was gardening. Sometimes Denise and I would walk over to the park and play on the swings and round-abouts and, when we could see Mr. Scott packing his tools away, we would run across to him. He would put us both in the wheelbarrow and push us all the way home. That was great fun especially at harvest time when the new carrots and peas were pulled to take home. We would sit and munch them, not too many because we knew they were grown to take home to feed the family.

We were now growing quite fast and getting stronger with our ideas and as we were left to our own devises sometimes we went too far with our projects.

In 1942 the government decreed that all old iron and scrap metal was to be collected and sent to the war effort. The rag and bone man didn't ride on his horse and cart any more because there was nothing left to collect. All the rags which once would have been thrown away were now used to make fresh clothes to wear and the remnants were turned into dusters. All the scrap metal was collected by the council workers and turned into ammunitions and guns.

One afternoon my Mother returned home from work to find her nice chain link fencing around her front garden had been removed by the council workers to help the war effort, which left her garden open to all the stray dogs (there were quite a few roaming the streets!). People were turning their dogs out on to the streets because they could not find enough food to feed them. They would run around in packs, some of them were hungry and became ferocious. Dogs had to be licensed which cost 7/6d (seven shilling and six pence) and money was short in the family budgets.

The garden looked so bare that she decided to plant some privet hedging around the outside wall. She was very pleased with the look of it so she planted privet hedge all the way down the one hundred and fifty foot side garden at the back of the house. She must have forgotten that she would have to cut it all several times a year when it grew!

At the bottom of the garden was a garage where my Father's car was kept. He had bought it from one of his friends before he went into the service as he had nowhere to keep it whilst he was away. It was a fawn Austin Seven which was now supported on bricks to keep it off the ground and hopefully protect the tyres until the return of my Father. My Mother occasionally cleaned and polished it to keep it looking good for him when he returned!

Two prized apple trees grew in the middle of the garden. One was a James Grieve and the other a Cox's Orange Pippin. Both were attractive looking apples and very tempting when they were ripe. I knew that my Mother sometimes counted them to make sure we didn't go "scrumping". Potatoes and runner beans were growing in the centre of the garden and "Dig for Victory" was the motto of all gardeners. She worked hard in the garden both on wet or dry days. On wet days she used to say, "I'll have a path down this garden one day."

Because the ground was very muddy for her to walk on to put the washing out on the line at the bottom of the garden, I thought that I could help her to build a path. One sunny afternoon during a school holiday I rounded up as many young friends as I could and asked them to go around the street and pick up all the loose stones, put them in a bucket and when their buckets were full they were to stand at our back gate and when my Mum came home from work she would give them all three pence for each bucket of stones they had gathered.

I could never understand why my Mother was so ungrateful to me for my help in building her a path. Twenty of my friends had gathered buckets of stones for her to help her keep her feet dry in wet weather. Where did I go wrong? In hindsight, she didn't have enough money to pay my friends. That thought never crossed my mind. But she did keep me busy for the next few days digging out the path and filling it with stones!

Whilst I was digging out the path one afternoon I heard a strange noise which sounded like a car engine. I knew it wasn't a car because no one had a car on the road as petrol was rationed. I looked up into the sky and saw a strange aeroplane with two sets of wings, it was hovering above me. I ran into the house to alert my Mother who ran out to see it with me.

"That is a reconnaissance plane, taking pictures of us all from the air, one day people will travel in those all over the world".

CHAPTER EIGHT
THE REALITY OF WAR

The Anderson air raid shelter had been assembled in our garden and sunk into the ground. Two neighbours decided the job could be done much easier if they all helped one another to put their shelters up. They could be placed in any direction so the three men decided to put theirs in opposite directions. This would prevent all three shelters being out of operation should one of them be bombed then at least the other two would be usable. Good thinking, except that the water table was not taken into consideration! The first heavy rainfall we had proved that we all had a problem. The bottom of the shelter was then one foot deep in water. We had to bail out with a bucket and throw the water some distance away otherwise it would run back in to the shelter.

We were supposed to sleep in the shelter when the bombing became heavier. There were two iron bed springs which were supposed to support Mum and me but neither of us fancied sleeping in the shelter with water on the ground. We felt that we would be just as safe sleeping or sheltering under the kitchen table.

Now that the shelter was practically unusable Denise and I thought of a wonderful game of catching newts and frogs with a jam jar tied around the neck with string. Dicing with death, neither of us thought of the consequences if we fell off the bunk bed frames into the water, which by now was over three foot deep and neither of us could swim! We never learnt to swim at school because all swimming lessons at the town baths had been stopped. The doors had been closed until the war was over.

This war seemed to be going on for a long time. For two little girls everything seemed the same, except for the air raids but we had grown used to them. We knew what to do and when to do it. Finding games to play, something to eat and somewhere to go, was all that worried us. Something to play led us into all kinds of situations. Something to eat was a real problem. No longer could we help ourselves to doorsteps of bread and thick butter topped with chocolate spread which was always available. Biscuits never materialized when Mum came back from shopping and somewhere to go was also out of the question. We both had to stay near home in case of an air raid, which rarely happened except for one afternoon.

The air raid warning had sounded and I was alone and sitting in the front room which overlooked the Avenue and across into the house opposite when I heard a very loud rat-a-tat-tat, I ran out the front door only to see two aeroplanes chasing each other round and round in circles. One of them diving down towards our Avenue aiming machine gun bullets at two young people as they were walking along. They ran into a doorway and I disappeared back into the house. I had witnessed a 'dog fight' between an enemy Meshersmitt 109 and one of our Spitfires.

I didn't know whether to run into the shelter but decided not to because they could have seen me and I would be sprayed with bullets. They were trying to shoot each other out of the sky. I was very frightened. What would I have to do if one of the aeroplanes fell to the ground, even on the house? Would I be buried under all the debris? Machine gun bullets were sprayed in the road, I was too frightened to go and collect one, for me the war had started. I kept watch on those bullets and when I felt it was safe I joined several other children from the surrounding houses hoping to collect one as a souvenir. Sadly the boys had collected them before I could get one.

On dark winter evenings I used to walk to the hospital to wait for my Mother to come off duty. I admit that I was scared but I waited beneath the dark yew trees and, when I heard her footsteps, I would let her know I was there with my torch shining on the ground. She used to say, "Jean darling, I wish you wouldn't come to meet me. It's so dark for you standing under those trees".

We linked arms and began to walk briskly home. I felt that somehow she must be feeling lonely and she needed my company, I never thought about the danger, I had a role to play now that my Father was in the war and that was to protect my Mother and give her as much support as I could.

My own safety never entered my head, I was developing a thick skin and I was ready to take on all that faced me, this was war and I was ready to play my part as young as I was.

Because we could not use the air raid shelter due to the water, we had to think of another way to protect ourselves. Mum told me that the safest place in a house was beneath the staircase. We did have a cupboard under the stairs where the gas meter was fixed to the wall and she kept a few shillings stacked on the top to put in the meter when the gas ran out, but it was so small there really wasn't room for two of us to sleep in there. She had the brainwave of turning the huge kitchen table in the dining room into an indoor shelter. It really was enormous and very strongly built, how it ever came into the house I'll never know. It definitely was a farmhouse kitchen table which would have kept us secure until help arrived if we needed it.

I thought this was a wonderful idea because we could have the fire alight all night and keep ourselves warm. Mum said no, that was not a good idea because if a bomb dropped on our house the fire coals or embers would be thrown across to our bed where we were sleeping. We would be cooked to a frazzle before any help came to pull us out of the debris. Once I thought about that, I realised Mum was right.

Our only form of heating in the house was the coal fire both in the dining room and the front room. There was a box curb in front of the fire with two side seats which housed paper and sticks in one and coal in the other. It was such a cosy place to sit on winter days, toasting slices of bread on a toasting fork. We had to be very careful with the number of coal fires we had. Coal was rationed. The industrial areas were the first to get the allowance but after that ordinary households were able to get theirs.

Meat from the butchers shop was rationed and we were issued with meat coupons. We needed to register with a butcher which ensured us that he would have enough meat carcases in his refrigerated room to supply all his registered customers. Some items were not rationed and often we enjoyed some rabbit pie, or tripe and offal which was off ration but made extra tasty meals for us. Mum used to buy beef dripping which we used to spread on toast, we could have it thick with salt sprinkled over it. We would have a cup of Bovril with it (tea was rationed and so was sugar, these were kept for week-ends). Occasionally another meal we enjoyed was tripe, she would stew tripe with onions and make a lovely supper for us both. Chitterlings made another tasty meal (these were pig's and sheep's intestines which were part of the offal allowance). We had to queue a long time to get them and as home refrigerators were not available in those days, we had to eat them as soon as we bought them because they would not keep too long.

We had paraffin heating stoves which we could put in the bathroom to warm it up on bath nights. It was either me or my Mother that would have to walk to the main road to get the paraffin can filled up. We could have a gallon at a time which would keep the heater going for a few days in the cold weather. The regulations that we lived with stated that baths should not be filled deeper than five inches. Our hot water came from a gas Ascot water heater down in the kitchen but we had to have a window open to let the fumes out. All very well in the summer but not so good in the winter.

Cleaning teeth had to be done in half a cup of water. We always had trouble with frozen pipes, ice sitting thick on the outside water drainpipe. Mum and I regularly climbed up the step ladder outside the house to pour hot water over the ice which collected in the drain pipe to try and release the water to flow through the taps inside the kitchen. On several occasions we had a burst pipe. Water sprayed everywhere and we had to bandage the pipe, turn the water off at the point at which it came into the house and wait for the plumber to come and mend it.

The winters were harsh, we could always bank on snow for Christmas! We enjoyed the slides the big boys built outside Denise's home. She lived in a Cul-de-Sac which was quite safe as far as traffic was concerned. There was very little movement by private transport, only the Doctor had enough petrol to run a car The slides were quite long and I held on to Denise as we sped down the slide and ended up on our bottoms falling about with laughter. We built snowmen in our

55

front gardens and dressed them with stones for their eyes and sticks for their noses and mouths. Sometimes they were standing in the gardens for weeks before the warmer weather arrived.

The Christmas post arrived in big trucks and was delivered to the houses by students on holiday from colleges. Everyone was in a festive mood when the post arrived. On days when my Father's letters arrived, my Mother used to run upstairs with them and I knew better than to ask her questions. She could now read quite well. She always told me that 'he sends you his love'. In fact, in hindsight, I knew very little about his war-time experiences, probably because he couldn't tell us much due to the censor cutting out any references to the war!

We were both getting along very well. Really there was no need to have my Father around! We never knew where he was. He had devised a system with my Mother before he went away that he would change her initial on the envelope when he addressed it which would spell out the country he was in. It seemed to work, she was quite sure that he had landed in North Africa early 1942. We wondered if he was in Field Marshall Montgomery's eighth army in the desert, but when he came home he told us that he was with Field Marshall Alexander and stayed with him throughout battles in North Africa and Italy.

My Mother had to be very careful about the items she wrote to my Father during these times. The air raids were continuing and our other cities were being bombed. Docks and harbours, cities, factories, railways and all kinds of transport were being attacked. The Germans were trying to bring our country to a standstill. She could not write about these things otherwise the censor would have cut her letter to pieces in case this information fell into the wrong hands. Suspicion played a part in the war years. Trust no-one she told me, you never know who is listening.

CHAPTER NINE
THE BEST OF INTENTIONS

My Mother decided to keep a few chickens. She thought that the eggs would be useful because, as they were rationed, she never had enough of them to use for her cooking and she liked to bake cakes and a few extra eggs would help to feed us. A chicken shed was built for us by a neighbour with a promise from my Mother that she would give him some eggs now and again. A run of wire netting was attached to the shed and it all looked professional. All we needed was a few hens!

My Mother bought a few laying hens from the gardener at the hospital where she worked. He kept quite a few hens in the hospital orchard. I occasionally went with him to feed his chickens and collect the eggs. We eagerly awaited the arrival of two Light Sussex and two Rhode Island Reds and of course the eggs! The groundsman arrived the following day. He had fixed a wooden crate to the handlebars of his bicycle and the chickens were delivered to us. We stood and watched as they strutted around in their new home.

A few days later one egg arrived in the nesting box in their overnight shed. It was a lovely brown egg, but which one of us would eat it? We decided to wait another couple of days to see what happened. Sure enough we received a gift of two more eggs, another brown one and one white one, this meant that both breeds were laying. We shut them up in their nesting area at night to keep them safe from foxes. We would open them up in the morning. By the end of the week we had six eggs in a bowl in our kitchen.

We became quite attached to our hens and decided to white wash the inside of the hen house to make them look clean and tidy, it would also cut down the risk of disease from chicken muck. Soon I found it was my job to clean out the chicken mess and put it at the bottom of the garden to be used as fertilizer for the vegetable patch. Not forgetting her promise to our neighbours we both walked to

Aunty Betty's kitchen door with three lovely eggs in a bowl for her with a promise of more to come.

Denise, Mum and me in front of the chicken run

Auntie Jennie was the next neighbour to receive a few eggs. She wrapped four of hers into onion skins and tied them around with string and boiled the eggs a little longer than normal as she wanted to make sure the eggs would be hard boiled. When they cooled she unwrapped the onion skins and the shells were coloured and the lines showed a pattern where the string had been wound around the egg.

Rearing one day old chicks was my Mother's next project. The chicks looked so pretty, little balls of yellow fluff on two legs was how I would describe them. They were kept in an old wooden drawer which was ideal because it gave them some strutting room and, as they couldn't fly, they were quite safe. In the summertime they would stay outside in the sun with some wire netting over them but in the winter they came indoors to keep warm.

My Mother treasured her chicks, just like a Mother hen, Auntie Betty called her. She was a good hearted neighbour but she did gossip and it wasn't long before the neighbours knew all about my Mother raising day old chicks. In the winter months she devised a way of keeping them warm when she went to work because it was dark when she came home. They were now growing feathers so it would be such a pity to lose them at this stage. She built a platform over the gas stove where the chicks in their box enjoyed the warmth of the gas flame beneath them.

One afternoon when I came home from school I could hear the chicks making a noise in their box. They were obviously feeling cold. It was another hour before my Mother came home so I thought I would put them on their shelf over the gas cooker to keep warm just as my Mother did, I had often watched her build the primitive incubator. First the bricks then the box, I put several layers of newspaper in to soak up their mess and put the box over the gas burner leaving it low just as my Mother did. Denise called for me to go to the shops as her Mother needed some shopping I brought her into the kitchen to show her what I had done.

"Will they be all right while we go up to the shops" asked Denise.

"Oh yes," I replied. "My Mother does it all the time when she has chicks to rear".

Turning the key in the back door off the two of us went to the shops. The hospital where my Mother worked was quite near the shops and I thought it would be a nice surprise for her to have us

59

both walking home with her, giving her a bit of company, so we waited together in the dark under the trees for sight of her coming down the drive. Denise didn't like the dark trees and wanted to go home. I tried to reassure her she was quite safe with me. Soon I heard my Mother's footsteps but as I didn't have my torch with me I called out quietly to reassure her that there were two of us to meet her.

We were all laughing and chatting happily as we walked home along the Avenues when Mr. Blackburn, the shoe mender came cycling along on his bicycle. When he saw us he cycled across to us, out of breath, he said "Mrs. Hunt, there is smoke coming out of your kitchen window, you had better hurry because it looks quite serious".

We ran like the wind. What could it be? In horror I thought about the chicks in their box! As we neared our home we could see the smoke spewing from the kitchen window. We had a fire to cope with.

"I'll go and get my Dad to bring his stirrup pump over to help put the fire out".

Denise hurried as best she could struggling home with her Mother's shopping in her basket which must have been quite heavy.

We entered the house from the front door, my Mother made me stay outside as she went in to survey the damage. The kitchen was well alight, buckets and buckets of water brought the blaze under control. One baby chick had learned to fly and was sitting on top of the kitchen cabinet no longer cheeping but croaking. All the others had died in their box. Mr. Scott did not need to use his stirrup pump because by the time he arrived my Mother had extinguished the fire.

Denise had gone home with her Father and I was sitting in the armchair sobbing. My Mother didn't get cross with me. She realized that I had tried to help her with the incubator but I had forgotten one very important piece of equipment to build it, an iron tray, which sat between the bricks and the wooden box. I never dabbled in rearing baby chicks again. As for my Mother, she got out the tin of paint and before long the kitchen looked as good as new!

My Mother saved all her vegetable peelings to feed the chickens and cooked them in a large pan. The smell was dreadful, I always found something outside to do when she was cooking the peelings. I went to Denise's home. We could usually find something to do. She had a lot of jig-saw puzzles which we both enjoyed putting together. We also liked colouring books and magic painting books.

The chickens needed bran to be mixed with the cooked peelings, corn to make the egg yolks rich and grit to make the egg shells. All these items had to be carried from a corn/seed merchant in Watford, six miles away. As we had no transport and there was no delivery service it meant two little girls would walk easily one way and stagger back home carrying seven pounds of either Bran, Corn or Grit at least twice a month. We didn't mind, but we did put our brown paper bags down for a rest occasionally. We made sure we went on fine days which meant we didn't have to cope with soggy packages.

When the chickens stopped laying, they were very old and had to be killed. There was a very good meal or two for both of us. Mum would first of all select the birds that were to be killed. At first the hospital gardener would come on his bicycle to wring their necks but after a few months my Mother did this job herself. She would hang the dead chickens in the garden shed to drain the blood from the bird, then the plucking of the feathers began.

Plucking was quite an art, taking the feathers from the bird without tearing the skin was a skill that both of us learned after a few bad attempts. Once the feathers were off the bird they were put in a large brown bag and tied up with string and baked in a low gas oven to kill all the insects that had collected in the feathers over the chicken's life-time. The feathers used to make me sneeze as the dust got up my nose. We both put handkerchiefs around our faces to protect ourselves.

Once the feathers had been cooked the bag was left to cool. Probably the next day we would undo the string and sort them, those that were too big were thrown away, but the small ones were kept to fill our pillows. My Mother had a feather mattress on her bed which was lovely, soft and very warm. Eventually this was the mattress that we brought downstairs and put under the huge dining room table to sleep on during the air raids.

My mattress was hair filled. I slept well on it. It never occurred to me that it was filled with horse hair. I would have been very upset if I had known but like everything else at that time it was taken for granted that all was well and no questions were ever asked.

We kept chickens until the end of the war and we lived well from them. The neighbours actually paid us for the eggs after a few months of getting them for free.

CHAPTER TEN
GOOD AND BAD TIMES

Our lives conformed to a regular pattern. Up at eight o'clock, wash in the bathroom, (fine in summer but freezing in winter, when we were lucky if any water came through the taps at all), we often had to boil a kettle to get enough water to wash with; breakfast, and off to school. I returned in the afternoon to an empty, cold house in the winter. From four fifteen to six fifteen was always a mischievous time for me. I planned and thought up ideas on how to amuse myself until I walked to the hospital to meet my Mother and walk home with her.

It was not so bad in the summer months but it was awful in the winter especially when the snow was on the ground and the ice stood a foot high on the outside water tap. My Mother taught me to knit when I was quite young and I became good at it. I used to enjoy working out patterns and over the years I knitted several jumpers and cardigans for myself. Knitting wool was on clothing coupons and I used to put eight ounces of wool on my birthday or Christmas list, colour was not important because you had a very limited choice from the wool shop. I also enjoyed embroidery, "Penelope" transfers could be ironed on to plain fabric and with the transfers came the guidelines as to colours of silks and wools suitable for the stitches to be used on the designs.

At eight years of age I could turn the heel of a sock knitted on four needles and my school teacher was so impressed that she sent me around to all the classrooms to show the classes what I had achieved. At that early age I was quite embarrassed by this and spent half an hour in the cloakroom passing time away before returning to my class-room. My needlework was also admired. When I went into senior school my needlework was sent to an exhibition in London, It was never returned, neither did I receive any commendations.

Our next door neighbours were very good to us. I know that Auntie Jenny (not my real Auntie) would keep a watchful eye on me

63

until my Mother came home from work. She didn't get involved in war work because she had small children to look after, but her husband (Uncle Joe) was in the army and he was sent to Burma. Aunty Betty and Uncle Reg (again, not my real relations) often invited us into their home to play cards during the week-end when my Mother was not working. They were both too old for either war work or joining the forces although Uncle Reg was in the Homeguard. I was quite good at cards although I was only eight or nine, I learned a lot from both of them.

We played Newmarket which was a card game. We played for pennies and halfpennies I thought it was fantastic to come away with some extra coins. My pocket money from my Mother was six pence a week but I couldn't buy sweets because of rationing, I didn't go shopping very often.

Uncle Reg had a fantastic stamp collection and there was nothing I liked better than to sit by him and look at the coloured stamps from all over the world. They were all mounted on black paper and the writing was in white ink. His album was very impressive. He would wear white gloves on his hands before he handled any of his stamps. I was not allowed to touch them. I started to collect stamps of my own and very often I would spend my pocket money on a large packet of stamps which would keep me occupied for hours. Try as I might, my displays never looked as good as Uncle Reg's.

Sometimes my Mother would invite them back to play cards in our home and when it was my bedtime she would put two armchairs together and I would climb into them, she would cover me with a blanket and I would fall asleep whilst they continued to play cards. They are very happy memories for me.

Denise was my very best friend and we used to amuse ourselves during the cold winter afternoons and at week-ends when my Mother had lit the fire in the dining room. We spent hours poring over our games. My Mother was either washing clothes or baking in the kitchen. We played at Post Offices (our favourite game) we used to design our own postage stamps, make our own envelopes and glue together pads of writing paper.

64

Another game we enjoyed was shops. We would use my Mother's weighing scales complete with weights which she used for cooking and we lined up all her packet foods from the cupboard, made our own ration books and weighed up all the imaginary groceries we needed to buy. If we played this game while she was at work, she would come home and find all her cupboards ransacked, and many spillages on the kitchen floor. This was not always appreciated as she had rag mats (made from heavy weight materials such as old coats, skirts or trousers, which would be cut into strips about one inch wide and eight inches long and hooked into a piece of sacking which created a very nice kitchen mat) all the spillages would be trodden in during the afternoon game. But she never complained. I think she must have worried a great deal about having to go off to work leaving me to my own devices for six hours every day. On occasions when the air raid warnings sounded she must have worried herself sick over me, but Denise and I never worried, it was the normal way of living and we got on with it.

One afternoon we decided to make a little house in the cupboard under the stairs where the gas meter lived. I remember we had two cream crackers for our food! We barely had room to turn around when the air raid warning went off.

"This is the safest place in the house" I said, feeling very brave, hiding my real fears of terror from Denise.

"I think I ought to go home" replied Denise.

We could hear the aeroplanes overhead. There were several planes droning above us so we shut the cupboard door to shut out the noise and to make ourselves safe until the all clear sounded.

Denise started to cry, "I want to go home. If I'm going to die I want to be with my Mum".

I remembered the machine gun and the bullets, and how they bounced along the avenue.

"You're safer in here with me. You're not going to die, I won't let you!"

I was trying to think about what I had to do if a bomb dropped on us and we were buried in debris without letting Denise know how afraid I was.

We started to sing some songs from the school choir. After half-an hour the all clear did sound and we breathed a sigh of relief, but to our horror we found that the door was shut and the catch to open it was on the other side of the door. We had to stay there until my Mother came home from work. She was delighted to see us when we called to her to open the door to release us. She said she had been so worried about us during the air raid.

"You two are amazing. There I was worrying about you when the siren went and here you are as if nothing has happened" she gave us a hug, Denise ran off home and we sat down with a cup of tea.

Denise and I decided to join the Junior Library which was some two miles walk away from our homes. We completed the forms and our Mothers signed them for us and, feeling grown up, we walked across to the Library. We handed in our signed forms and we became members. We were introduced to the Junior Library section of the main Library. All those books! I can remember my thrill at seeing books that I could take home to read and it didn't cost anything at all. Occasionally on Saturday mornings the Library put on some attractions for the members of the Junior Library. I can remember on one occasion we saw a puppet show – that was wonderful, all for free.

During our walk to the Library we passed an Automobile Association telephone box which members belonging to the A.A could use if they had problems with their cars. The box was painted in black and yellow and it stood on a little hill. I was very proud of that box because my Father belonged to the A.A and every time he drove his car on the road, if he met an A.A patrolman riding his motor bike with a sidecar for his tools to repair broken down cars, the A.A man would salute us as we drove along the road making us feel very important.

Now we were in war-time and my Father was fighting the war in another country, I was walking alone to the library. I passed the A.A box when a convoy of army vehicles full of soldiers passed me. I stood and watched the soldiers who waved to me. Suddenly, a dispatch rider on a motor bike drove around the round-about straight in front of an army vehicle. The rider was badly injured and when the army helmet was taken from the head I noticed that it was a woman with her blonde hair tangled in blood.

From that day I realized, as young as I was, that women were now playing their part in the Army and in the fullness of time our own Princess Elizabeth (now our Queen) joined the ATS, the Women's section of the Army. They were not on the front line, but playing a very important part behind the scenes, supporting the main war effort.

During the school holidays we had to think of things to do. Sometimes life was miserable if Denise and I had fallen-out. Luckily it didn't happen very often. In hindsight those times were very valuable in later life, a good friendship should be treasured and ways of sorting out grievances should be discussed, not allowed to linger, making both parties unhappy. As children it seemed like the end of the world without your best friend.

Playing street games like Hopscotch using the markings on the slabs to mark out the numbers one to ten. The game could be played as a team game or with two people, all you needed was a flat stone which would you slid along the pavement into the number you needed to get, from one to ten. Hand-stands was another form of achievement, you needed a secure place on the ground to put your hands on and then throw your legs up over your body to support yourself with your feet resting on the wall. This game lost its attraction as the girls grew older.

Boys took on the challenge of conkers. This game was played in the autumn when the horse chestnut trees threw their fruit to the ground after a strong wind. The shiny brown nuts were collected and the biggest ones were pierced with a skewer and a string was threaded through and knotted at the end to stop the string pulling back. The game was to hit your friend's conker as hard as you could which would either split it or knock it out of his hand in which case you would win. You either threw his conker away or kept it if it was in good condition.

Climbing trees was another experience to learn from. I loved climbing up as far as I could go and feeling safe. Collecting sticky buds in the spring and placing them in a vase, watching the sticky buds turn into full horse chestnut leaves was a good nature lesson. On one occasion I stood on a branch that must have been rotten inside and I fell to the ground. I went home with a split lip, bruised face and grazed knees.

Picnics were some of the best times we had. To pack up your food for a day and walk off into the fields was a wonderful feeling of freedom. We could stop where we wanted, or go as far as we felt was far enough. Denise and I usually made for a fun spot called Otters Pool. We never actually saw an otter but what fun it was to wade into the water with our dresses tucked into our knickers with a jam jar and fish net on a pea cane to catch whatever we could find. We would spread our food on the grass. It always tasted so much better than from the kitchen table. A bottle of lemonade and two cups, (no plastic in those days). We had no fear, sometimes other children sat a few feet away with their picnics. We walked home with a jar full of tadpoles and bright rosy cheeks from our day in the warm spring sunshine.

On the way home we walked passed the railway tunnel through which flowed a stream which was full of frog spawn and newts. Our jam jars were filled with both as we waded into the dark tunnel. When we arrived home we got an old tin bath and put some rocky stones in it, filled it with water and emptied our jars of newts and frog spawn into the bath. For days we watched and waited for the tadpoles to emerge from the frog spawn. When they turned into bigger frogs we would take them over the fields and watched them hop away. We needed to give up our walks when the gypsies camped in the far fields. They tied up their horses to trees and their dogs ran all over the fields barking at anyone who came near. Their fires billowed out smoke and their washing was hung from the trees and spread out over bushes. It was all a bit scary!

The war was gradually intruding into our lives. My Mother's Mother came to stay with us for a few days holiday. We thought that she needed a break from the air raids. She lived in Southsea which was heavily bombed night after night. We went to meet her from her train in London. I liked my Grandma Thorburn. She would read to me and play board games while my Mother was at work. I loved listening to her as she had a Scottish accent which fascinated me. She went back to her home after a few days because she was worried about leaving it un-attended during the air raids. She had two daughters living close by her in Portsmouth, my Aunts Janet and Helen.

The air raids were getting more frequent again and there were several during the night-time, one after the other. The sirens would sound and my Mother would get me out of my bed and we would sit together downstairs and listen to the gun fire. Sometimes we could hear the whistle of a falling bomb. Then there were big bangs and we would say, "Someone's getting it tonight". In the morning we would still have to get up and go to school. The pictures of the bombed buildings were printed in the next daily paper.

Our school lessons were held in the long corridor because it was considered the safest place for the children to be. The classrooms had big windows which, although they were covered in brown sticky tape, would give horrendous injuries to the children if they were blown in. It was decided to bank up sand bags in the school corridor and allow us to sit with our backs to the sandbag walls. There must have been two hundred and fifty children at any one time, all between seven and eleven with five teachers. Each class teacher had a small area in which to teach their particular lesson.

One morning the air raid warning went and we all had to sit with our heads between our knees. We heard the drone of an enemy aeroplane above us (you could tell the enemy aircraft due to the engine noise), then one almighty bang. Some children were screaming and others were crying. Teachers were trying to pacify those that needed comforting. I watched as I was well used to sitting up all night with my Mother but this was a big bomb and made a horrendous noise as it fell through the air on to target, which was meant to be our school! After a few minutes we all looked up and sighed with relief. The bomb had fallen on the farmhouse behind the school. A few days later we were all taken to the farm to see the crater the bomb had made. We were not allowed to go too near because the farmhouse was gradually falling down. The school playing field was now out of bounds. School sports-day was cancelled due to the fact that the children were vulnerable to enemy aircraft. There would not have been enough time to reach the safety of the school building to be sheltered from the overhead aircraft.

Anti-aircraft guns in parkland
Imperial War Museum N.H143

Soon the American armies arrived in Europe, mostly in our country. Aeroplanes and men arrived in their thousands. They had a lighthearted attitude to the war, but they soon learned. Dances were arranged by the American troops. They brought the "jitterbug" which livened up the lives of our women. Children were fascinated by the American soldiers who always had a supply of sweets in their pockets. Chewing gum was every child's dream and a little ditty emerged from those days, "Got any gum, chum?".

The air raids were more frequent now, more at night than day. Sometimes we went to bed under the kitchen table and listened to the gun fire. We heard the bombs whistling as they travelled through the air. If the raid was in the evening, my Mother would take me out into the garden to watch the searchlights sweeping the sky. They were looking for enemy aircraft. Sometimes we saw a silver speck in the beam and then the guns would fire trying to shoot it down before it dropped it's bombs on a near-by town.

Anti-aircraft guns were placed in the parks and on open areas. Barrage balloons were secured to concrete blocks on the ground and floated in the skies to catch enemy bombers. If they flew into the balloon it would explode as it was filled with gas which would kill the pilot and the aircraft would fall to the ground.

A Barrage Balloon made ready for release
Imperial War Museum N.A6172

All these installations were surrounded by barbed wire to safeguard them. When the guns fired at aeroplanes they sounded so loud, they were deafening. Sometimes bombs fell and didn't explode, that was scary. We sat and waited for the thing to blast us all to kingdom come but the army came and removed the detonators from the bombs and made them safe and left the bomb where it had landed, to be removed later.

One afternoon my Mother came home from work, made a cup of tea, sat down in the armchair and lit a cigarette. I was horrified to see this and asked her, "Why are you smoking?"

Her explanation was that because she was working in a hospital, she was picking up germs and as she didn't want to be ill she felt that smoking would kill the germs. Shortly after that revelation Denise and I sat on the box-curb and we sampled this smoking to see what happened, I screamed as the cigarette I was smoking was stuck to my lips and burning my mouth – I never tried it again!

CHAPTER ELEVEN
A WAY OF LIFE

The eagerly awaited letters arrived from my Father. His system of changing the initial on our address worked. Sometimes his letters would have holes cut out of them. My Mother would shout "Oh no" as she drew the precious pages from their envelope. The Censor had cut out all the comments written by him relating to where he was and how he was moving around with his vehicle, making the page almost unreadable. After a while the letters arrived with indelible ink blotting out words, which was much better because the reverse side of the writing paper was left intact.

As the envelopes arrived we were able to piece together the name of the country he was fighting in. It was North Africa. When we didn't receive letters for a few weeks, we knew that he was on the move and all the letters would arrive together from wherever he had been sent. Then the initial game started all over again. We dreaded the brown official War Office envelope which relatives received when their loved ones had been killed in action. Thank goodness we never received one of those.

During the latter part of the war we received aerogram letters. These appeared to be small photographed sheets. Letters which had been written on normal size notepaper were reduced by photographic means to save paper. At that time the soldiers could not get writing paper due to the shortage of newsprint. The aerograms took far less space and were sent home by air making the contacts between families much quicker. I received an aerogram for my 10th birthday. My Father had drawn a camel walking under a palm tree with the words, Happy Birthday written on it.

Life at home continued with much the same routine. Denise and I had joined a Sunday school held at a local Church and, on Sunday afternoons, we walked together, crossing a main road quite oblivious of danger. We felt quite grown up. My Mother instilled upon me never to speak to strange men. Now that we were at war, it was even more important to understand that not everyone was your 'friend'. There didn't seem to be many air raids on Sundays which gave people a chance to rest and make up some sleep to get ready for the next onslaught which we knew would come.

There were now a great many wounded military men back home. Some had to find work even though they had been injured and were not fit to rejoin their military colleagues.

Salesmen started a door to door selling scheme. We had a man selling for Kleen-e-zee, a brush manufacturer, another man sold larger items which normally we would have to have permits to buy. One man came to open his case on our doorstep showing a range of expensive tea-sets by Heat-master. The teapot was encased in bright shiny metal which kept the tea hot, doing away with a tea cozy. My Mother liked that and asked him to call back next week when she had her pay-day.

During that week she was in touch with the Mutuality man. He was a money lender who agreed to advance her the money she needed at an agreed repayment amount. The tea-pot stood on the sideboard together with the milk jug and sugar basin all bright and shiny, I never recalled it ever being used but I do remember the Mutuality man calling for his money every Friday until the wretched tea-set was paid for.

My Grandma and Grandad Hunt were still living in London during the bombing. My Grandfather worked as a runner for the admiralty which meant he would walk or run between government offices delivering or collecting important messages. (No mobile phones or computers then.) After the nights of heavy bombing, the primitive telephone lines were all disrupted and important messages needed to get to the right people quickly.

During the weeks of the blitz my Grandma Hunt was sent to live with us for a short while but my Grandad remained in London. His work was important. He knew his way around Whitehall and after the night's bombing nothing looked the same the next day.

Fires were still burning but the important offices were underground, he could get the messages to the right people, and take the replies back to their sources.

Because of the night bombing my Grandad was not allowed to go back to his home in Finsbury Park. He had to sleep in the London underground stations with thousands of other Londoners. Sometimes he was lucky enough to get a bunk bed but mostly he slept on the platforms. The spirit of the people was all good natured and they shared what little they had with each other. Grandad was safe with his food as he was fed by the government when he returned to the offices.

The W.R.V.S (Womens Royal Voluntary Service) would serve tea and sandwiches to the people sleeping on the platforms. The trains were stopped overnight because they never knew if the railway lines would be bombed disrupting their services next day. But they were safe from the heavy bombing so the people did get some sleep. The women would emerge from their sleep in the early morning, walking up the stone steps leading from the underground station platforms, looking around them at the devastation that had been caused by the overnight bombing. Some of them had no homes left to go back to. There were some escape miracles, people were pulled alive from the rubble after being buried under heavy concrete for several hours.

I didn't like my Grandma Hunt living with us. She disturbed our routine! She was profoundly deaf and had to wear earphones to listen to the wireless, that and the daily newspaper were her only pleasure. This meant I had to maintain a delivery and collection service for accumulators to keep the wireless going and collect the newspapers every day.

She did the crossword in the morning, lunch-time she would listen to the wireless (Workers Playtime introduced by Bill Gates) this was a programme broadcast from factories across the country and for one hour, they were allowed some entertainment during the war workers lunch time. She used to laugh so much the tears would roll down her face.

Her favourite programmes were "ITMA" with Tommy Handley, he was a comedian, and later, it was "Have A Go" with Wilfred Pickles, this was one of the first quiz programmes to be broadcast by the B.B.C. "In Town Tonight" was a topical programme introduced by Eric Maschwitz. The sound of London Traffic in Trafalgar Square was brought to a standstill by Eric shouting "Stop" and he would interview people in the news and famous celebrities that were in town that night.

Queuing became a national pastime. Every commodity you could think of was either rationed or on coupons. We would queue at one shop for butter and sugar, another for meat, and another for vegetables and fruit if we were lucky. I can remember on one occasion Auntie Jenny (from next door) shouted at me over the garden fence, "Jean go up to Colliers (the greengrocers) he has got a box of oranges. He allows one per person but be quick, you will have to queue and he hasn't got many left".

I was lucky, and that evening I sat with my Mother enjoying half an orange.

Your ration book was marked when you had bought the allotted amount of butter or sugar. The coupons were cut out so that it was impossible to use them again.

There were times when stolen goods and produce came on the market. There was often someone who knew someone who could get this and that off coupons or rations. And there was always someone who wanted to buy a little extra at any time but the prices were exorbitant. This trading became known as "The Black Market". It was an offence to deal in this way and if anyone was caught they might be imprisoned.

People were good natured through these times. Shopping for food could take hours.

Flying Officer Thomas H. Morgan (USA) Pilot

A sobering thought in a quiet Lincolnshire Village

i

Picture of the Vatican and stamps
.
Father's gift to me on his return from the war

Denise

Here we are today, sharing some of our war-time memories with you.

We are still the
best of friends.

Spring 2010

Jean

Legal Tender King George: V £5.0.0d Note. Gold Sovereign = £1.1.0d.

(One Guinea). Gold Half-sovereign = 10s.6d. Crown = 5s.0d. Silver Florin = 2s.0d (two shillings).

Silver 3penny piece

1 FARTHING	¼ OF ONE PENNY
2 FARTHINGS	= ½ OF ONE PENNY
2 HALF-PENNIES	= ONE PENNY
3 PENNIES	= THREEPENNY PIECE
6 PENNIES	= SIXPENCE
12 PENNIES	= ONE SHILLING
24 PENNIES	= TWO SHILLINGS
30 PENNIES	= HALF- A- CROWN
120 PENNIES	= 10 - OR ONE TEN SHILLING NOTE
240 PENNIES	= ONE POUND NOTE
5 ONE POUND NOTES	= ONE £5.00 NOTE

DECIMAL (15TH FEBRUARY 1971)

2 HALF-PENCE	= 1 ONE PENCE
2 ONE PENCE	= 1- 2 PENCE PIECE
2 TWO PENCE+	
2 HALF PENCE PIECES	= 5 PENCE
2 FIVE PENCES	= 1-10 PENCE
5 TEN PENCES	= 1 - 50 PENCE
10 TEN PENCES	= £1.00 COIN
2 £1.00 COINS	= 1 - £2.00 COIN
5 X £1.00 COINS	= £5.00 NOTE
2 X £5.00 NOTES	= 1- TEN POUND NOTE
4 X £5.00 NOTES	= 1-£20.00 NOTE

GENERAL INTEREST

CONVERSION TABLE FROM OLD TO NEW MONEY 15TH FEBRUARY 1971

CHAPTER TWELVE
A RISKY BUSINESS

We received a letter from my Aunty Janet telling us that my Grandma Thorburn's house had been bombed in Southsea. She had been taking cover in a street shelter when the air raid warning went. She was well and unharmed but had moved in to live with Auntie Janet until she found somewhere else to live.

Mum thought that she needed to go and see her Mother and we should make the journey to Portsmouth as soon as possible. She went to the railway station to work out how we would get there by train and the times the trains would run providing there were no air raids. It seemed that it would be possible to go there and back in a day provided we started out very early in the morning.

On the 19th of August 1942 we set off for Portsmouth at six o'clock in the morning and travelled to Euston station in London. We then had to walk from Euston to Waterloo to catch the train to Portsmouth. So far so good! The walk along the Euston Road was memorable. Burned out buildings, rubble everywhere, sandbags piled high along the road, no traffic due to pot holes from shells and falling buildings. People were walking quickly to get from or to their destinations in case there was an air raid.

Soon we entered the station concourse filled with soldiers, some sleeping on their rucksacks, mostly sailors waiting for our train to take them to join their ships in Portsmouth harbour. Getting on the train was no problem but getting a seat was impossible, the noise was bedlam, everyone in good humour making the most of their free time. Sailors were playing cards, smoking cigarettes and drinking beer. The atmosphere was thick with smoke, but there was nowhere else to go. We had to stand for the whole journey.

When we arrived at Portsmouth station we were met by my Aunt. She told us the bombing had been so heavy that we would have to walk to wherever we wanted to go because all the tramlines had been destroyed by bombs and shells. When we walked out of the station we could not believe our eyes. The only building left standing was the City Hall which seemed untouched. The bombing had reduced all the other buildings around the City Hall to rubble.

We set off to go to look at Grandma's bombed house. When we arrived outside I remembered the milkman with his horse and cart standing on the cobble stones outside the front door. The little house had been one of six terraced houses. All seemed to be standing secure but, when my Mother opened the front door, we looked down into a crater which had been the sitting room, the frontages of all six houses were supporting one another, but the bomb blast had taken the backs of the house down and into the crater.

Where was Cherry Boy? and the gramophone? All gone, there was nothing left standing, just memories. All three of us shed gallons of tears that day. She closed the door gently and we turned and walked away.

We arrived at the house where Aunt Janet lived and found that Grandma had been moved to live with her other daughter Helen. We would not have time to go and see her as the walk was too far. We had a cup of tea and a chat, relieved that Grandma was safe. Some families were being split up because it became difficult finding accommodation for several people. Families wanted to stay together and moving into someone's home became very difficult. By the time a letter had arrived in the post with a new address, there was another air raid and everything changed again. This happened to my Grandma's other daughter. Aunt Helen's house had a direct hit one morning. Fortunately they had all gone into the street shelter and after the raid they had nowhere to live.

Whilst we were having tea with Aunty Janet before returning home she asked us if we could put up an evacuee. How could we take anyone back to live with us? We were miles away from each other!

"Who?" asked my Mother.

My Aunt left the room and returned with the most adorable dog on a lead.

"Meet Jimmy," she said.

He had been bombed out. Both his owners had been killed in an air raid and my aunt had looked after him but she could not continue to feed him,

"Could you take him home with you?" she asked.

"Yes. Yes," I said. I had always wanted a dog but how would we get him home?

Between us we devised a carrying bag and wrapped 'Jimmy' in a blanket. We could not afford to buy a ticket to get the dog back home on the train. Aunty Janet gave us seven and six pence to buy a dog licence and off we went back to the station. Fortunately the dog only weighed five pounds. He was a pedigree Pomeranian.

We were travelling on a day return ticket which meant that we had to be on the train to London by a certain time. It was just getting dark as we were walking back to the station when the air raid warning sounded. We could see the station but we also saw the enemy aeroplanes flying towards us. We began to run towards the street air raid shelter. When the bombs started to fall and the machine guns began to fire, someone took hold of me and threw me into the shelter, I was caught by a warden. My Mother followed with the dog in her carrying bag.

A bomb fell opposite the shelter and we all felt the shock but no-one was hurt. We had to wait for the all clear before we could continue our journey to the railway station. The air was full of dust and fires were blazing along the roadside. We didn't have much time to think about what was going on. We wanted to get away from this carnage. We joined the train standing in the station. There were no seats. It was packed with servicemen coming from or going to their units. We held on to the dog very much aware that we had no ticket for him. It would mean a fine if the ticket inspector caught us.

The enemy aircraft were following our train as they knew it would be travelling to London. We stopped in a station to avoid them. The driver was trying to stop leading them to our destination. While we were on the train two soldiers gave up their seats for us and were concerned about the movement in our holdall.

"What's in there?" asked one soldier

79

We opened the bag and "Jimmy" poked his head out. All the servicemen around us were fascinated by our little dog. We told them the story of how we had acquired him and that we were worried as we had no ticket for him.

When we arrived at Waterloo station we held our breath as we neared the ticket inspector checking all the tickets as we passed through the barrier. The two soldiers were wonderful. They kept the inspector talking as we passed through the barrier. We waved good-bye to them and quickly walked from Waterloo to Euston station. We bought a ticket for the dog for the last lap of our journey which took the worry from us. Our remaining journey was free of any air raids but we wondered whether we had a home to go to. Soon we were walking down the road with the dog on his lead as if we had always had a dog! He had travelled so well and kept so quiet that we had completely fallen in love with him.

Next morning the news-announcer read out that there had been a very heavy bombardment of Portsmouth yesterday (which we knew) and that it was believed to be in retaliation for the raid on Dieppe. Our aeroplanes had bombarded the port of Dieppe across the channel and the enemy planes had followed our planes as they returned to their home bases. They raided and bombed Southsea as well as Portsmouth harbour.

CHAPTER THIRTEEN
GETTING IDEAS

A few days later, after the day trip to Portsmouth, I decided to give some thought to our very own first aid group that would enable us to help injured people if a bomb fell nearby. It could come at a minute's warning. No one would know what to do or how to administer first aid. I was going to set up a group for emergencies!

Denise and I gathered various small bottles from our Mother's cupboards together which could be filled with sterilized (boiled) cold water which could be used for cleaning wounds. My Mother always used boiled water for cleaning my cuts and bruises and if she knew what to do, it must be right. We also found a roll of cotton wool which we rolled into small balls to be used with the boiled water for cleaning wounds. Bandages had to be made from strips of clean white cloth from pillow cases or bed sheets. I knew where she kept these things.

We sat in the dining room making small bags, big enough to carry our first aid equipment and we put a draw-string cord through the top so that it would be easy to open quickly. We made the carrying bag from old pieces of black-out curtain material and to make it look official we embroidered a white cross on them. When we had finished we had made six bags. We commandeered several other girls from the Avenue to join our group. Each morning five or six little girls walked to school carrying their very own first aid bag all looking for unsuspecting patients. We disbanded after a week as no bombs had fallen and the other girls in the group left their bags at home!

We thought of another good idea. How about turning our garden shed into a week-day Sunday school. My Mother was not too happy about this idea but she knew that we had to amuse ourselves while she was out at work. Surely this idea was harmless enough. She finally agreed that we could take over the garden shed. We set about turning out all the garden tools, dusting the cobwebs away and cleaning the windows. We knew about singing hymns because we did that every Sunday but we didn't have any music. The giant iron wash-day mangle was the very thing. It was in the shed and if I could turn the iron cogs slowly and then quickly according to the rhythm of the hymn, I could accompany the congregation.

By careful arrangement of two wooden planks (used for decorating purposes) we had enough seating for eight people. We hand printed some invitations to a week-day Sunday school. The time of the service and the amount of collection money needed were clearly printed and given out to eight children living near-by.

The first week-day event took place and all the invited children arrived on time. My careful turning of the mangle drowning out their little voices singing their hymns. Readings were taken from the bible which I had found in a pile of old books that had been in the spare bedroom. The next event was arranged for three days time and hopefully they would all turn up again, but sadly, no! Once again another good idea had bitten the dust, but we still had the collection money which amounted to five pennies.

Our next idea was to turn the shed into a little house. Again all the cleaning took place, deck chairs were opened, and curtains were made to put up at the windows. We took off to the bakers shop and spent our five pennies collection money on some soda buns. At that time bread buns were not rationed. We walked the three miles home, made a hot drink in Mum's kitchen and sat down in the deck chairs to enjoy our soda buns in our little house.

My Mother would make sandwiches and leave them on the table in our little house for us to eat if we grew hungry. She made us a plate of beetroot sandwiches. These were Denise's favourite. She could slice bread so thinly that it would blow away in a puff of wind. She would cook the beetroot that she had grown, slice them very thinly and put it between two slices of dry bread. Sometimes she made lemonade and she would leave a jug out for us. We also made Ginger Beer which we grew from a plant. It wasn't a plant that grew in the garden, but a mixture of ingredients from the kitchen cupboard left in a jug to ferment. Water was added after the fermentation period had matured. It made a very nice cooling drink in hot weather.

During the school holidays Jane, a niece of Aunty Betty and Uncle Reg, came to stay with them for a short holiday. She had no one to play with so I went along to see if I could play with her. I liked going to Aunty Betty's because some times she made some rock buns or jam tarts and would give me one or two on a plate with a glass of lemonade. On this particular afternoon Jane suggested that we play hospitals and we put our dolls into their cardboard box beds and dressed up in our nurses' uniform to pretend we were in a hospital.

Uncle Reg's air raid shelter was a dry place, no water in his! The whole shelter was covered in climbing plants and in the summer it was a mass of colour but we were not allowed to go into the shelter. Jane had spied a couple of deck chairs that would be nice for us to sit in. Carefully she lowered herself into the shelter and handed out the two chairs to me. They were folding chairs like you would see on the beach at the seaside. Although I had never been to the sea-side, I had seen pictures of deck chairs in books. She arranged my deck chair and as I sat in it, it collapsed and trapped my hand in the side supports, my little finger was shredded from skin and I ran home screaming. Under the cold water tap went my hand and a nice soft bandage was put around it. Somehow my Mother always knew the right thing to do. Even to this day I have a crooked little finger on my right hand.

Our next idea was to get a few friends together and form a concert party. The air raids had stopped as the fighting had turned from the air to the ground. Our armies were at the front of hostilities in Africa and Italy. This war was going on too long and we were now getting bored. We could give a concert to all the other children in the nearby Avenues who would come and watch. We practiced dancing and singing and learned poems which we could recite. All this was done in our back garden on a cement area outside the French doors leading to the dining room. This would make a good stage area. We could change in the dining room and come through the door onto the stage area. When we felt that we had practised enough, we realized that we were short of costumes for dancing.

I knew that my Mother had a drawer full of nightdresses that she had lovingly made and embroidered ready for when my Father returned from the war. Surely she wouldn't mind if we borrowed them, after all, we were giving a concert to cheer our friends up while this war was going on. I ran upstairs, threw open the window and threw out all the nightdresses. There must have been a dozen, all colours, clean and pressed ready to be worn, but not by us!

We were all enjoying ourselves so much practicing our singing with the popular song of the day:

> You are my sunshine
> My only sunshine
> You make me happy
> When skies are grey
> You'll never know dear
> How much I miss you
> Please don't take my sunshine away.

We were prancing up and down the garden rehearsing for our grand opening that we never heard my Mother come home from work. She stood in the door way, her face was ashen. All the singers and dancers dispersed quickly to the safety of their own homes whilst I was sent to my room, awaiting my Mother's wrath after she had finished collecting her precious nightwear from all parts of the garden!

I never gave much thought to wash-days. They happened every week, but there was one particular occasion I will always remember. Our kitchen was very small and the washing was all done in a copper boiler. The water was heated by gas, not piped gas but through a hose connected to a gas tap and fixed to a burner under the copper. On Mondays my Mother always did the washing in the evening ready to hang out next morning if the weather was fine. In wet weather it would be hung on a clothes horse around the open fire. She used a soap powder called Oxydol and in the last rinse she would use a blue bag for her white garments. All bed linen was white. The smell of wet washing indoors permeated through the house. It was a soapy smell. It faded as the washing dried but there was dampness around the house for some time.

Washing and cleaning aides were quite primitive in those days. Washing up dishes was all done by hand without washing up liquid. We used hot water to which we added a small knob of Soda, this was to cut the grease, then Lux soap flakes, or a shake of Oxydol or maybe green soap swished around in the water. The hot water and soda would make our hands red and sore. We would suffer in the winter months from chapped hands or chilblains. Vaseline was the answer for our hands. Household rubber gloves did not come on to the market until much later.

On this particular Monday evening she told me to get on with my knitting as she wanted to shut the kitchen door leading to the hall. This would stop the dampness from the steam from the wash boiler bringing off the wallpaper around the house. During the evening I could smell an unusual smell and as I opened the kitchen door looking into the steamy kitchen I saw my Mother on the kitchen floor! I opened the back door and ran to get help from Auntie Jenny, next door. When we ran back to help her she was sitting up and propped against the kitchen cupboard, the draught from the back door had brought her round.

Auntie Jenny turned off the gas tap and put the kettle on to make us all a cup of tea. We realized how lucky we had all been because the rubber tube connected to the gas copper on to the gas tap had come adrift and the gas had affected her. She had no sense of smell. We could have had a gas explosion and we would all have probably lost our lives. These were dangerous times we were living through before modern aides made living so much safer.

Ironing was done on our huge kitchen table which was the main table of the house, as well as serving as a dining room table. Everything was done on it, from cooking to wallpapering. It really was enormous. Where it came from or how it was lifted into our home I'll never know. My Mother ironed on half of the table. Preparation of the ironing table began by laying an old blanket over the area to be used. Next, a clean sheet was put on top of the half that she was going to use. Her linen, which had been starched, was dampened, rolled up and placed on a neat pile ready for ironing.

The irons themselves were two flat irons placed one on top of the other over the gas burners on the kitchen stove. When the iron was hot enough to use it was necessary to test the heat by wetting your fingers and quickly tapping on the bottom of the flat iron, if it hissed then it was ready to use. This was quite a task, walking back and forwards into the kitchen, replacing the used iron on the gas stove and taking the freshly heated one back to the table. At the end of my Mother's ironing session, she would leave all the handkerchiefs for me to iron. No paper tissues and no electric irons in those days.

Mrs. Scott used to heat her flat irons and wrap them in a blanket and place them in Denise's bed on cold nights. I had a stone hot water bottle, it was the shape of a bottle with a washer and screw top, the hot water from the kettle was poured into the bottle, the stopper was screwed tightly to stop the water leaking in to my bed. Whilst it was hot it was lovely, I would put my feet in the warm space. Sometimes I would wrap an old shawl around it and cuddle it but when it went cold I used to push it to the end of the bed.

CHAPTER FOURTEEN
ENVIRONMENTAL MATTERS

The arrival of the school nurse would cause concern in some families. Class by class we were lined up for our regular inspection. Hair was parted, plaits were undone and a complete inspection for nits was carried out. I was one of the lucky ones that did not have to sit in class next day wearing a headscarf while the removal medication did the job it was meant to do.

The school Doctor's inspection was a different matter. Vests and liberty bodices were removed, stockings and socks came off and we would stand shivering in our navy blue knickers awaiting our full medical inspection when the nurse called our names. One by one, eyes tested, finger nails inspected, teeth poked and prised, feet checked and measured (if you were lucky you gained an extra allowance of clothing coupons if your feet looked as if they needed bigger shoes), height measured and then, if there was anything left of you, you were weighed.

Getting dressed in double quick time resulted in the remainder of the day spent in garments back to front! First you had your vest next to your skin, then the liberty bodice. This was a difficult garment to put on. It was like a jacket without sleeves, made of white cotton material with a kind of fleecy lining. It had rubber buttons down the front with button holes on the other side. The bodice covered the area from your neck to your hips and from that length hung suspenders to hold up your stockings. This was the first item of clothing that was left off when the warmer weather came. There was an old adage that said, "Ne're cast a clout until May is out," ten year old girls weren't waiting that long, if the sun came out that was good enough for us, regardless of the month!

During these early years of my school life I had my share of childhood ailments. Chickenpox covered me with hundreds of large red itchy spots which I was told not to scratch because they would leave marks on my skin for the rest of my life. I was made to wear gloves at night time because that was the time the itching drove me mad. I was awash with calamine lotion which dried to a white powder covering each spot. Gradually the chickenpox disappeared and I was as good as new (except for one hole in my forehead which remains there to this day). Measles were awful, a high temperature and restlessness and being kept in a darkened room for days but, thanks to my Mother's good nursing, I had no lasting effects from Measles.

Smog was another fear we all lived with. Due to the amount of coal burning, from industrial factories, and buildings set alight by bombs, combined with the smoke from household chimneys, smoke would collect in the atmosphere. When the dampness came during the months of November and December the smoke particles hung in the atmosphere causing fog. It was so thick it choked you, making you cough, in fact we used face masks to filter the dirt from the air we were breathing. The masks were white when we put them on but they turned into a mud colour by the end of the day. Thousands of people suffered from Bronchitis and died from respiratory diseases during these dreadful times.

After heavy bombing raids the smell of cordite hung in the air which was putrid. The fog became a hazard to drivers who lost their sense of direction. Accidents were caused by poor visibility. In the middle of the day the sun never penetrated through the fog and the air became colder than normal. We welcomed a strong wind which was the only answer to clearing the smog.

A few years after the war there was a Clean-up Britain campaign. The Government passed a "Clean Air" bill to keep the centre of London smoke free. Coal fires were replaced by gas fires and electric fires were installed in homes. The trains running in and out of the London stations were adapted from steam to electricity which meant the houses alongside the tracks were then free from smoke. The health of the people gradually improved when the smog disappeared.

In conjunction with this campaign the buildings in London City were water washed with high power water jets through hoses bringing back the original colour of new stone. The transformation was amazing, people would stand and stare at buildings that had always been black and depressing, which were now bright with a twinkle from granite when the sun shone on it. The London railway stations were transformed from sooty glass and blackened walls to bright shiny glass and coloured walls appeared to have been renewed, but of course they hadn't it was the washing away of the years of soot. In recent years the concourses at railway stations have been re-laid with marble which has made the stations very impressive.

Following on from this campaign garden bonfires were made illegal and house coal fires were restricted to smokeless fuel which was produced at the mines from coal-dust. Coke from the Gas Companies which were now producing electricity could be bought by the sack and, when there was a miners strike, people collected their own coke to keep their fires burning. Our fireplace was fitted with an "All-night" burning stove, which, if banked-up with coal dust, would burn slowly through the night and when the knob on the ash-pan was turned it would produce bright flames, which was fantastic at breakfast time on a cold winter morning.

Electricity was becoming a main source of power. Homes became transformed. No coal fires, but electricity cables were laid into peoples' homes enabling them to use electricity for heating, lighting and new home equipment that was to come in the future. Cables covered with conduit were channeled into the walls of houses then plastered over and the three pin plug arrived in the home. Out went the flat iron and in came the electric iron. One thing that made a difference in our lives was the wireless, no more trouping up to the shoe menders shop to carry an accumulator home so that we could listen to the news. We had a new radio which was powered by a three pin electric plug which had been plugged in to a socket in the wall behind the radio. What a difference that made.

We could get two programmes, the Home programme was for government notices, news and current affairs. The Light programme was for entertainment. Music all day long mixed with comedy shows in the evenings. The popular shows like workers playtime and ITMA were continued with additional programmes which were introduced slowly. Programmes for education in schools, Music and Movement helped with physical education, religious programmes helped to liven up the morning assemblies with stories from the Bible, much better than listening to a teacher.

I used to listen to Childrens Hour hosted by Derek McCulloch, (Uncle Mac) a childrens presenter. Once a week we had a programme "Out with Romany" which I enjoyed. Romany would take us through our imagination into the woods listening for bird song and looking for animal footprints and giving us advice on what to do and what not to do in the countryside. One of my very few Christmas presents in 1943 was a book "Out with Romany", I read it over and over again.

"Books" leads me on to a waste paper drive which was arranged by the school teachers. The Government was asking everyone to save paper. Publishers were hard pressed to continue with full size newspapers. They cut their pages down to four for daily editions and their week-end editions were not much better. The teachers asked all the children to bring unwanted books to school and on one particular day we were going to place them edge to edge around the school playground to see how many we could collect.

This idea really caught on and for days before the appointed day, we were all taking books from home to add to our goal. I thought that as we had a lot of old books around the house, this was a good time for a spring clean. The spare room seemed full of them. We never read them. My Mother could not and they didn't interest me. What was the use of keeping them? I went to school on several days with my bundle of books. I believe my Mother thought I was going to bring them back after the day of lining up the books!

The children were very excited as the line of books quickly grew. We all shared the job of carrying them from the piles of collected books that were stacked in the school corridor. After a while everyone received a cheer as the line of books progressed around the playground. I felt very important as I also received a cheer. The line passed all round the school playground and out through the school gates to the main road. People who had no idea what we were doing came out of their houses to put their unwanted books on our line. The whole day was so successful that the local press reporter came and photographed our event. Then the council came with their men and removed the books and took them away for crushing. After that they were passed on to be pulped into newsprint and toilet rolls, both were in very short supply.

My Mother saw the picture in the paper and the write up with the reason we had all been collecting the books. Sitting me down with a cup of tea she asked me about the books.

"Did you take any from the spare bedroom?" She asked

"Yes" I replied, "They had been gathering dust and I thought I would help with the spring clean".

"Do you know what you have thrown away?" she asked.

"Old books" I replied suspecting I had done something wrong.

"Not any old books" she replied

"They were all your Grandfather's books. We were looking after them for him. One included a signed book by Captain Scott. Your Grandfather sailed with him on one of his expeditions. How will we tell Grandad what you have done?"

"I'll tell him next time he comes to stay. I think he will be pleased with me"

"I hope he will," replied my Mother.

Somehow the day of the book collection was memorable, but for the wrong reasons!

The day of the books had fired everyone's imagination at school. Denise decided to start her own library which was to be held in her Anderson air raid shelter. She thought it would make use of the "dug out". It was never used for the purpose for which it had been installed and it was dry. No water in hers! So we spent many happy hours arranging the books (that we had left), indexing them and making return slips, sticking them inside the front covers. We had gained all this knowledge because we had joined the lending library.

We sent notices around to all the children in the area informing them about our library which would be open during the school holidays. Denise had a lot of books which her sister had bought for her and I had a few which I was willing to lend her for her library including my precious "Out with Romany" book. We had quite a queue of children on our first day of opening but somehow our system failed us. The books that went out never came back including my "Out with Romany".

The line of books had been so successful that the "Authorities" decided to re-vamp the idea with "a Mile of Pennies". This was to raise money for the war effort in some way or another. This was arranged in a different way to the books. We had to encourage our neighbours and relations to come to the school and add their contribution to the mile of pennies, thus involving many people. We were sent leaflets to distribute to our neighbours and relations telling them of the idea, encouraging them to save pennies for the big day.

The designated day arrived, it was bright and sunny. The mile had been marked out by the caretaker. He had used the curbs for the route so as not to involve children walking on the roads. The children at school all put their pennies down first which enabled them to watch the mile grow – and it did! Relations and neighbours arrived and were welcomed by their friends. The time passed quickly and before long it was the end of the school day, sadly we had not met our target but we had made a very good effort. The Caretaker collected all the pennies in a wheelbarrow because the weight was considerable. The money was all put towards the war effort.

CHAPTER FIFTEEN
THE AWAKENING

The ground fighting was still going on in Europe but the air raids were less frequent. My Father was now in Italy and there were big battles raging there.

My Mother was keeping the two of us reasonably well fed. It must have been very difficult thinking up meals with such rations. Our chickens were still laying eggs. Meals were monotonous, vegetable stew, scrambled eggs which we made from egg powder if we did not have enough fresh eggs. Now we were using dried milk powder, not nice to drink but fine for cooking. Mashed potatoes were made from dried potato flakes. When our own potatoes were ready for harvesting, we really did enjoy them. Mum had great patience in scraping the tiniest of potatoes and she served them with a knob of butter for Sunday lunch. Bananas, now that leaves a bad memory. Dried bananas came into the shops. They were horrible. No yellow skins, the fruit was dried into a dark brown sausage, sticky and difficult to eat.

Our school milk was fresh. The Ministry of Food was concerned about the amount of vitamins the children were missing due to our poor diet. We were the future generation and there was a possibility that we would suffer from poor health in later life. A campaign was launched to collect rose hips from the hedgerows which would be pulped into rose hip syrup, a good source of Vitamin 'C'.

Early that autumn an army of children of all ages scoured the gardens and countryside collecting rose hips. We took them to school in boxes and jars which were collected and sent off to the factories to be turned into syrup. Slowly, during the autumn months the bottles of Rose Hip Syrup, along with concentrated orange juice and Cod Liver Oil were supplied to clinics and we collected our allocation.

The arrival of a dubious fellow called "Spiv" appeared on street corners, pubs and shady places. He seemed to be able to get supplies of rationed foods and items of clothing without coupons but it was all at a price! My Mother explained to me that he was getting these items on "The Black Market". He was accompanied by a man in a car who was on the watch out for a policeman. The car would help the two men to make a quick get away. We wondered how he got petrol to run a car, but then we realized, that was the business he was in, getting items that the ordinary people couldn't get. At first women were sceptical about buying from him but when he offered to get silk stockings his trade increased.

His image was that of a tall man with long, greasy hair, a trilby hat, long floppy jacket and baggy trousers, both hiding his contraband which was for sale. If he was caught selling on street corners then he faced a prison sentence.

At that time there was a comedian called Arthur English who made a name for himself on the radio copying the style of "The Spiv".

Denise and I continued to go to Sunday School each week and when we were ten years old we eligible to join the "Sunbeams". This was a small club for the older children. We were expected to sign "The Pledge". This was a lifelong promise to avoid smoking cigarettes and drinking alcohol. In return for this we would receive a bright shiny yellow lapel badge. Denise and I thought about this for a little while. We decided to sign "The Pledge" then we could wear the badge on our school blazer lapel. I am sure that "The Pledge" was soon forgotten but the yellow badge stayed on our lapels!

The Sunday School Christmas party was the highlight of the year. As Sunbeams, we were asked to organize the games. We had jelly and cakes for our tea and a few chocolate biscuits appeared which nearly caused a stampede. We were awarded our prizes for good work throughout the year. I was given a small pink book of wild birds I could expect to see in our garden. I learned a lot from that little book.

As well as being "Sunbeams" we also became "Lighthearts". This was a group of older girls who were capable of knitting and sewing unaided. We would meet once a week at Mrs. Wilson's home. She was a member of the Church of England. She thought that, if she could attract young women and girls to knit items for the armed forces, it would make a positive contribution to making the men more comfortable.

We knitted squares 8 x 8 inches to be sewn together to make blankets for wounded soldiers or for refugees from the bombing. We made shopping bags from the cardboard milk tops which we covered in raffia and when they were stitched together they became quite strong. These were sold at the Christmas Fair to raise money for Military charities. Because I was good at knitting I was given a Balaclava to knit for a soldier. I knitted gloves and socks amongst other items. Mrs. Wilson allowed us to use her home in the winter months but in the summer we used to walk two miles across the fields to have our meetings every Friday evening in the vestry of the local Church. This was our first introduction into our own Church life.

One afternoon in late spring we had a heat wave. I can remember the long hot summers we had as children. We could always rely on six weeks summer holidays from school living out of doors most of the time. But we also had bad storms. May was always a warm month and we were allowed to take off our liberty bodices and go into summer frocks but our Mothers had to add four inches of matching material to the bottom of our dresses because we had grown over the winter months. We felt good wearing our new ankle socks and white plimsolls.

I was playing quite happily on my own, as my Mother was home from work. It was early evening and the daylight lasted until ten o'clock. She called me from the dining room to come and see what she had to show me. I was surprised to see the boy from a couple of houses along the Avenue sitting in the dining room talking to her. He was holding a very large tin under his arm. She put her arm in the tin and drew out a great long grass snake to show me and came towards me with it. I knew nothing about phobias at that time but I soon knew I had one! I screamed the house down, ran upstairs and into the bathroom locking the door behind me. It was hours before I would come out, no matter how my Mother coaxed me or what she promised me or how often she said sorry. I would not go near her for days and it was months before I would trust her again. I made up a bed in the spare room for myself and even when the air raid warning sounded I would not open my bedroom door. I would not sleep with her under the table. She was very worried about me. From that day I knew I had a phobia and I have been terrified of those reptiles ever since.

Christmases were very sparse occasions during the war years. No-one felt very much like celebrating. Most families had someone missing, either in the forces or evacuated. I cannot remember having a Christmas tree in the house as a child. The first one I saw was around 1943/4, a silver paper one standing in a pot on top of the radio. I always had a Christmas stocking, sock was more likely. Mum would put a shiny penny and a few nuts in the toe, a rosy apple and if I was very lucky there would be an orange if she had been able to get one. A French knitting set or a yo-yo would complete the sock filling. Giving presents was only for the immediate family. There was no money for spending on other people. No one expected presents.

The School Christmas party was a highlight. We made paper chains for a couple of weeks before the party and the caretaker would hang them around the walls and fix them with a few balloons. Mothers would make cakes and jellies and we would play games in the afternoon before breaking up for the Christmas holiday period. We were allowed to take some of the paper chains or, if we were very lucky, a balloon, to brighten up our homes.

The Christmas story was well loved by the small children. There was a manger set up in the school hall where we sang carols. When we knew all the words a few of us would be daring enough to go carol singing at night-time. We were not allowed to carry torches so we had to learn the words and sing the right tunes. We didn't stay out long because it was cold and the darkness was inhospitable. Very often it would be snowing and the neighbours were wary of opening their doors.

We seemed to be very competitive in those days making tests for each other to prove our ability to succeed from nothing. No-one was spoilt. No-one came out to play with anything other than a skipping rope or marbles, dabbers (five stones) or hopscotch and there was a major investigation if you lost your skipping rope, firstly because it couldn't be replaced and secondly no-one could get another!

CHAPTER SIXTEEN
A LITTLE HELP

My favourite radio programme was "Children's Hour" it was broadcast between five and 6 o'clock every week-day. It was full of interesting reports bringing facts to children, helping them understand what was going on in the world. The presenter, known as Uncle Mac, (Derek Mc'Culloch) told us about the Russian people, how poor they were, and how they had been under siege from the German Army for weeks. They were short of food and clothing and we were asked to send donations to Mrs. Churchill's Aid to Russia Fund.

I thought that I could do something to help. I knew my Mother would not be able to send any money as she was finding it hard to manage for the two of us on her own. Her earnings were very small and after the rent was paid there was very little left and we needed every penny to live ourselves. My six pence a week pocket money wouldn't help very much. I talked my idea over with Denise and we set out to raise money for the fund.

No concerts, no Sunday Schools just a 2 lb glass jam jar on a piece of string! The jam jar was left over from the 1920/30s, the times when big families needed feeding and the 1 lb of jam on a loaf of bread was not enough to feed a family. I found the jar in my Mother's larder where she kept all her stored goods. Once we had tied the string around the neck of the jam jar we designed a collecting card informing people of what we were doing. Whilst my Mother was at work Denise and I walked around the area calling at houses collecting money for Mrs. Churchill's fund. We kept going for a whole week and gradually the jar filled up. On the Friday evening we could get no more money into it. It was absolutely full and very heavy. Coins in those days were much larger than those of to-day and heavy to carry in your purse or pocket.

After our evening meal that day I bucked up courage to tell my Mother what we had been doing that week. Her face went quite pale and she looked quite sad, turning to look me straight in the face,

"Jean darling, what have you done? What will you get up to next?"

I wasn't quite sure what she was going to say so I held my breath and waited,

"Now what are we going to do with this collection?"

"Count it" I chirped.

I was very proud of what we had done. All the money tumbled out of the jar on to the kitchen table and we started to count it. Piles of coins stood like soldiers, the total collected was £14.10.07d. Next morning we walked to the post office and handed the money over to Mrs. Hemming the postmistress. She gave us a postal order for the correct amount and we put it in an envelope addressed to Mrs. Churchill, 10, Downing Street, London.

Denise and I sat down and made notices to tie on to fences and lamp posts informing people of the total collected during our house to house collection. My Mother walked around with us and helped to tie the notices high enough so that everyone would see them. Imagine my surprise when a couple of weeks later I received a hand written letter of thanks from Mrs. Churchill addressed to me at my home!

To Jean

Envelope from Mrs Churchill

January 1943

10, Downing Street.
Whitehall.

Dear Jean,

Thank-you very much for your gift which I have just received.

I am most grateful to you for the trouble you have taken to help the brave Russians in their terrible struggle & in the glorious defence of their country.

Your sincere friend

Clementine S. Churchill

Letter from Mrs. Clementine Churchill

The South of England, especially around the port areas of Dover and Folkestone, had been badly bombed and the residents were having difficulty finding somewhere to live. The Government appointed inspectors to call on households away from the bombing areas to ask for the use of their spare living accommodation. We didn't want anyone else sharing our home but the Inspector came in and looked around and told us that we would be receiving a family from Dover.

A couple of days later the Inspector came back and this time he brought with him a family of four.

"I can only take one" my Mother protested.

"Yes, we know that," replied the Inspector, "but this family want to stay together. It will only be for a short time".

We understood that, so we took the Mother, but the two little girls (about my age) went to stay two houses along with Auntie Betty (everybody's Auntie). Arthur the husband looked drained, very pale and his skin had a sooty appearance. Not surprising when he explained to us that he was a coal miner in Dover and he had brought his family to get them settled before he went back to work in the mines. Mrs. Whittingstall, Barbara and June stayed with us for a couple of months. Barbara and June went to school with me and Denise each day and after a few weeks they returned to Dover where a house had been found for them.

A few days later we had an Irish man billeted with us. We were asked not to ask him any questions about his life or work. All we knew was that he had a family in Ireland. He wasn't very old. He was out all day and he was very quiet. One morning a telegram came for him. He had been called back to Ireland as his wife and five children had been killed in an air raid on Belfast. Poor man, he packed his bag and left for home or what was left of it. Belfast was another port like Dover. The enemy bombers tried to sink the ships that were in the docks.

We became used to having strangers staying with us. On another occasion the almoner at the hospital where my Mother worked asked her if she could help a family who were in trouble. They had travelled from Cornwall to be with their daughter needing an operation. The Father would return to Cornwall but the Mother wanted to stay near her daughter so that she could visit her little girl but she had nowhere to stay. Mum took her in for a few days. Mrs. Jeffries came to stay and slept in the spare room.

After the operation the little girl recovered well enough to return home to Cornwall by train. My Mother was asked if she would accompany Mrs. Jeffries and her daughter in the ambulance to the London station. As the ambulance could not wait to bring my Mother home it would be necessary for her to return by train. She agreed to do this and packed a few things in a bag next day for her trip to London in the ambulance. I would have to spend the whole morning on my own. I was given strict instructions by my Mother on what I could and couldn't do. She promised to bring fish and chips back with her for our lunch.

All went well at the London station, the little girl was transferred from the ambulance to the train and the ticket inspector came to collect the tickets and agreed to allow my Mother to sit with Mrs. Jeffries until the train was due to leave. The guard blew his whistle to send the train on its way and my Mother walked to the door to get off the train only to find the door was locked The train drew out of the station with my Mother on it, no ticket and no way of contacting the guard.

She called from the window for help but the train was well under way to the next stop. As the journey to Cornwall was a long distance, the train did not stop for a couple of hours. When it did stop the ticket collector came looking for my Mother. He had been told what might have happened to her at the London station. That was why she didn't have a ticket and that she didn't have enough money to buy a return ticket. He kindly put her on the next train back to London.

The hours went by and I was waiting for my lunch, the only thing in the larder to eat was an egg which I boiled. Eventually around six o'clock my Mother walked in the door without fish and chips, exhausted!

"Where are the fish and chips?" I shouted, "I'm hungry".

Obviously she had been very worried about me as I had been on my own for a full day. There was no way she could contact me. She couldn't let me know what had happened, no phone or mobile in those days. She burst out laughing and over a cup of tea she told me about her day.

CHAPTER SEVENTEEN
WAS THE STORM OVER?

In 1944 the war news took a turn for the better and the country was feeling more optimistic about the future. For days now the army vehicles full of troops had been travelling along our main road both day and night. Everyone was in an expectant mood. The soldiers were laughing and waving to us as we stood queuing for meat at the butchers shop.

"Something's up," said the Butcher. "They've been going along the road all night."

"Second front," shouted a man from the queue.

We sat eating our lunch glued to the radio as the announcer reported that on the 6th of June, D-Day, there had been an invasion by the British and American Armies on the French coast.

The air raids had stopped and we were beginning to relax. We were getting a good night's sleep. However, the skies took on a sinister invader, the doodlebug! This was an unmanned guided weapon. It had the shape of an aeroplane with a tail of fire. It had the noise of an engine. When the fuel ran out it would drop from the sky to the ground without warning. You could see it with a tail of fire then you would be filled with fear as the engines stopped, then you realized that if you could see it, it was going to fall very near to where you were.

Air raid sirens were of little use against these weapons. We never knew where they would stop and drop. We really did live in fear. They would come in the day-time as well as the night. As I was on my own while my Mother was at work, each time one came overhead I can remember saying a little prayer to myself. I curled up in a ball in the armchair, put my hands over my ears, held my breath and waited! One night a doodlebug fell on a group of houses not too far from where we lived. Forty eight people were killed that night as they slept in their beds.

The Menacing VI "Doodlebug"
Imperial War Museum N. CL3433

The factories and sites where these dreadful weapons were being assembled and their launching pads were found and our aircraft smashed them to smithereens. But the Germans were not to be out witted, they had an even more vicious weapon. It was known as the V2 Rocket. It was shaped like a huge cigar.

The Dreaded Rocket V2

Imperial War Museum N.BU11149

Devastation of Sandringham Road
By kind permission of Mrs. Greville

They too were guided by remote control, no wings, but it was silent! They were really terrifying. I can remember one falling in the park a quarter of a mile away from where we lived. Luckily it was at night and no one was in the park at the time so there were no injuries. It left a huge crater which left nothing to the imagination of the amount of damage it would have done in a built up area. We were an inquisitive group of youngsters and we wanted to see where this weapon had fallen, but the park was out of bounds for a few days. When we were allowed back into the park the area was roped off and there was nothing to see but the crater.

Our local authorities decided it was safe enough to open the cinema on a Saturday morning for the children's entertainment. It was great. Denise and I walked the mile and a half with our sixpences in our pockets. We had three pence for our ticket and three pence for our bag of chips when we came out after the film. The chips were not rationed but the chip shops were controlled as to the hours they were allowed to open. We didn't mind standing in a queue for our bag of chips. We put salt and vinegar on them and enjoyed them on the way home!

The films we saw were in black and white but we didn't mind. Laurel and Hardy made us laugh, Roy Rogers always caught his man and Lassie always came home. We forgot about the war for a few hours. There was a talent contest one Saturday morning and I went with a friend. We were dressed as two Dutch children and sang "I'm a Little Dutch Girl and you're a Little Dutch Boy". We didn't win but it was fun, dressed up and standing on the stage in front of all those children.

I was nearing my tenth birthday at the end of the year and my Mother thought that I ought to have something special as a celebration now that the air raids seemed to have finished (although we were never quite sure about that). Our next door neighbour, Auntie Jenny, asked me if I would like to go to a London theatre to see a show as a special birthday treat. I was very excited about this and I hoped my Mother would let me go. She agreed so we were booked to see Ivor Novello's "The Dancing Years". The theatre was just off Piccadilly Circus. We were to go by train which, after changing on to the London Underground, would take us to a stop just outside the theatre.

I saw all the sleeping accommodation on the platforms which had been used as the air raid shelters. When we came up the steps, out into the open space it looked quite frightening. Buildings were only half standing, there were piles of debris along the road-side and all the statues were surrounded by wooden boarding to protect them from the bombing. Where there were fountains, barbed wire was filling the trough where the water should be to stop people climbing up the boarding to look over the top. I could just see the top of Eros behind the wooden boards.

Most of the famous statues in London had been removed and taken to the country for safety. It would be lovely to see them all come back when the war was over. The bombing had decimated London but a couple of theatres were still producing shows for the public to see. The most famous one was "The Windmill" and they boasted that they never closed even though they received a direct hit by a bomb.

This day I was to go inside a London Theatre for the very first time. It was breathtaking. Rows and rows of seats not just on the ground but there were several balconies all very ornate in their gilded paintwork and red upholstery. The chandeliers hung from the ceiling with their lights twinkling and all around the balconies were small lanterns reflecting light from the chandeliers. It was hard to believe that there was a war going on outside the front doors.

The stage was hidden by enormous curtains. An orchestra played as the scenes changed and the singing of the soloists was memorable. The costumes were really spectacular. I was completely over-whelmed by it all. When the last curtain fell we had to get back to the station as quickly as possible as it was now dark. There were no lights in the streets or along the roads. That was the time for air raids to start if there was going to be one.

We regained the nervous anticipation that we had been living with for a few years. The expectation of the sirens, searchlights and fires made us run to the station for the train. We were in the centre of London, no lights anywhere but thousands of people going about their daily task.

There were no air raids on the way home and the wonderful memories of that day have stayed with me for years. When I arrived home I was greeted by my Mother with a wonderful birthday surprise of a doll's pram. It was not new, but it was something I had always wanted, a dolls pram of my own. It was two tone light and dark brown and the covers and pillows were made by my Mother. There was also a doll sitting in the pram. She wore a sewn dress and knitted cardigan made by my Mother. I couldn't wait for her to need some shopping because it would give me the opportunity to show off my pram and doll. And what's more, I could bathe this doll as she was made from rubber.

My Mother had arranged for us to be photographed. Now that the war was drawing to an end the letters to and from my Father were no longer being censored. I had grown up so much that she thought my Father should see a picture of me. Films for cameras were very expensive and hard to obtain and processing them was even more difficult. That was why she made an appointment to go to a commercial photographer. We had decided to take Jimmy with us for a good walk because we would have to walk ourselves. It was about four miles to the studio and fortunately the weather was good.

We opened the door of the studio and the bell rang as the door closed. From the end of the room, which was very dark, the photographer came through parted curtains. I felt that he appeared mysteriously. He wore glasses and he had a stoop but he was very nice. He spoke to us and suggested that the dog should be in our photograph, I was delighted about that and his mysterious appearance didn't worry me, in fact I began to like him even more.

Colour photography was new and very expensive. All studio photography was in black and white or sepia. My Mother chose sepia. We were posed in various settings and Jimmy was perfect. He did everything he was told. My Mother was very brave due to the fact that she had recently had all her teeth removed and was struggling to talk and smile with her new teeth in place. She explained this to the photographer and he understood her difficulty. He decided to make the pose semi formal which would not require my Mother to make a full smile. I did likewise and Jimmy didn't smile at all.

The photographer stood behind a large brown box which stood on a tripod, with a black material cover over his head. He must have taken our picture, but I never heard any click or noise of any kind. He threw the cover back over his head and said, "That's done Mrs. Hunt, if you like to come back next week the pictures will be ready for you."

The following week all three of us walked again to the photographer's studio to see the finished results. We were highly delighted with the pictures. My Mother sent off the picture to my

Father who was still in Italy, knowing full well that he would receive it and it would not have been censored by the British Field Post Office.

Our very own evacuee

It was now nearing the time in school when I would be taking the eleven plus examination which would determine the remainder of my school life. I was not brilliant at school but I was a good average veering towards the arts side rather than academic. The mixed classes were suffering from the disruptive influence of boys, doing what boys are good at in creating havoc in the lives of the girls. But there was one boy I really liked. His name was Peter but all the other girls liked him too. I did have an advantage because he lived close-by me and he would always talk to me when he passed by which made me feel special, but this didn't last long after he kicked a football through a plate glass panel in our front door!

My Mother continued to work at the hospital and we were approaching the long school holidays. The weather had become very warm, in fact most summer holidays could be relied upon to be warm and sunny. I continued to walk the dog to meet her from work after I came home from school. He was a great companion to both of us. These days I could only get into the kitchen when I came home from school. She knew that it was daylight and warm and I very often went out to play after I had eaten my bread and jam so it was not necessary for me to have the run of the house. I usually did my homework until it was time to set off to meet her. The hall door was locked to stop me ransacking the house. We had both learned our lessons when it came to accessing private rooms!

One particular Friday I walked home from school with Denise and I was feeling very poorly. I didn't go out after I had made myself a cup of tea, in fact I didn't drink the tea, I was definitely unwell. I curled up on the kitchen floor with the dog beside me. I cannot remember anything more. Later that week my Mother told me what had happened: As I was not in the usual place to meet her from work with the dog, she thought I had gone to the shops and forgotten the time. When she tried to open the kitchen door she had difficulty because I was on the floor leaning against it. She went around to the back door which was open and when she saw me she knew I was very ill with a high fever. She carried me up the stairs and put me to bed and called the Doctor who diagnosed Scarlet Fever. He said that I should have been sent to the isolation hospital at the other end of the town but, as my Mother seemed to be a very good nurse, he would leave me in my bed and he would visit me every day until the fever had subsided.

On the sixth day I was able to be bathed and my Mother had made me a new nightdress. It was Lilac in colour. She had embroidered small flowers around the neck line while she had been sitting by my bed for six days. When I felt better, all I wanted to eat was a bowl of soup, which wasn't difficult, we lived on soup! I was in bed for six weeks.

Denise would call in to see my Mother each day. She brought get well cards that my companions had made at school which my Mother arranged around my bedroom. Six weeks is a long time for a ten year old to stay in bed and day by day I was feeling better and stronger. My Mother asked for schoolwork to be sent home for me to keep me occupied. I knew that by now I had missed the eleven plus examination and that I would have to go to the Secondary Modern School. I was heartened to know that not many of my friends had passed the examination. At least I would have friends around me when I started my new school.

One afternoon, when my Mother had returned to work, towards the end of my convalescence, I was so bored that I decided to make some home made sweets. When Denise called in on her way home from school I could give her some. Mum made these sweets and they were delicious so I looked in her cupboards and found the ingredients icing sugar, cocoa, margarine and dried milk. I mixed it all together then rolled small balls into the icing sugar and set them out on some greaseproof paper as I had seen my Mother do. I waited at the front room window to see Denise walking down the road. I opened the window and called her to come around to the back door as I had a surprise for her.

She looked through the glass to see the sweets. Neither of us had many sweets as they were still on ration and the sight of all these little chocolate balls was too much for her.

The back door was locked because my Mother would not leave it open whilst I was in bed. She went around to the French window in the dining room and climbed over a garden chair and in through the fan-light window and the two of us, for the first time in six weeks sat laughing and enjoyed all these little chocolate balls.

When my Mother came home I told her what I had done and that I had washed-up and put everything back in the cupboards but, when I told her about Denise's visit, she went quite pale, I thought, once again, that she was not pleased with me.

"I hope that you have not given Denise scarlet fever," she said.

I never thought about that, but fortunately no infections had passed on.

When I eventually returned to school I was told that I had missed my eleven plus examination. My Mother tried to get me a second chance to sit the examination but Mr. Judd the Headmaster said:

"No, Jean has to go to Secondary Modern School and take her chances there".

The final blow came when I was told that Denise would not be transferring to our new school with me. Because her birthday fell at the beginning of a new year, she would have to stay in the junior school a little longer.

CHAPTER EIGHTEEN
A NEW SCHOOL

The year was 1944, my very first day at my new school was daunting. I had to walk to school which was much further away from my home than my junior school. There were no buses in that direction. I had never seen this school and I didn't know where it was. I walked slowly behind some other children who were obviously walking in the same direction. I was told that I would have to walk two miles before I saw the school. It was about right, but suddenly in the distance I saw it. It was massive, a two storey school! My first impression was, 'Here's a challenge!'

I was looking over what seemed like miles and miles of allotments. I had to walk alongside these allotments until I reached the playground. There was also a massive playing field by the playground. The grass had been cut and marked out with white lines ready for the next set of games because this was the beginning of a new school year and here I was, alone, without my dearest friend Denise.

I walked into the school to be faced by large notices which read, "New School entrants go into the hall". Finding the hall was worrying, miles of corridors, nothing like my little junior school. A tall girl came up to me and showed me how to get to the hall. There were thousands of children and what a noise they were making – but – no boys. What had happened to the boys? I didn't realize that I was in a single sex school.

A tall lady with black tightly curled hair walked through the throng of noisy girls and up on to the stage and immediately there was silence. This lady was important. She was the Headmistress, Miss Clifford. The notices were given out and I waited for the one that suited me.

"All new girls to stay in the hall. Other girls to go to your classrooms."

I stayed in the hall. I looked around for a friendly face but couldn't see anyone I knew. All the names for each new classroom were read out, I thought that I had been forgotten until near the end when most of the girls had left. I looked around at my new class mates and I was horrified. Was I really going to be put in the lowest class with non readers? This was because I missed the eleven plus exam, I thought "I'll show them, they'll be sorry". And with this rebellious attitude I followed my new class teacher, Mrs. Burns.

At break-time I asked her if I could speak to her about my classification and I told how unhappy I was. I explained that I could read before my fifth birthday, I could write and do real writing before I was six, and I knew all my tables by rote. She was very understanding and explained that the report from my junior school stated that I had spent little time at school during the past year, "that is why you have been unclassified." I explained that as well as looking after my Mother when she had her teeth out I had also had a brush with death and scarlet fever. Her advice was to go back to my desk and she would get things sorted out within a few days.

Mrs. Burns was true to her word. A few days later there was a class assessment and due to the poor reading ratings in the class I was given my own reading group. There were five girls who were really struggling with their reading and together with patience, the six of us worked very hard on their reading and day by day their skills improved. I enjoyed this time and felt that I had proved my ability to gain the standard required to be put in a higher class. Sure enough, at the end of the term I was put into a higher grade.

During the September term there was an air raid warning. When the siren sounded we were all sent into the air raid shelters. This was a big school with hundreds of girls but it was obvious that this exercise had been well practiced over the war years and it was well organized by the teaching staff. The shelters were across the playground, under the nearby wooded area. They smelled very musty. They were damp and claustrophobic. I hoped that I would not be down there too long. The all clear sounded and like a herd of animals we rushed up to the fresh air. It was the only time we used the shelters. I think it must have been a practice incorporating all the new girls to make sure that they knew what to do in an emergency.

I mentioned earlier the absence of boys in our school. Their school was on the top floor above us. I continued to make steady progress in my class work and within the year I was in the second to top class. Denise joined the school the following year but, by that time, I was well adjusted and had made several new friends and was now in a higher class and beginning to start a second year. Although I was now in the higher grade I was devastated when the decision was made to send the group learning French to Paris for an educational tour. I was not allowed to go because I had not started to learn the language when I first arrived in the new school (regardless of how hard I had worked to better myself).

All the set backs I had suffered only fed my determination to succeed, no matter what I was doing, although I did not realize it at the time. I often received a few kind words from Mrs. Burns as she passed me in the corridor. Sometimes she would sit with me while I was knitting during break times. I found knitting very therapeutic. It was something I could do well. She asked me if I would knit her a cardigan, no mean task as she was a very large lady but I was happy to do this for her. When it was finished she gave me some pocket money which really boosted my morale. The staff room must have been discussing my ability because I received several orders for garments by other members of staff which enabled me to earn quite a bit of extra pocket money.

Needlework and Art were my best subjects and I excelled in both. My needlework went on show with an UNESCO exhibition along with my painting of a vase of lilacs. Both items were not returned to me, and no record of my achievements were noted. In my later school years I received prizes in both subjects.

In my class there were forty girls and from year two I made steady progress and at the end of year exams my class position steadily rose. It was my goal to be in the top five. New lessons appeared on our timetables; Domestic Science, Needlework and a little gardening! We also learned to cook and occasionally we were allowed to visit the Gas Showrooms for cookery demonstrations on how to use our food rations in a more interesting way. These subjects would be alternated giving us an insight into all the skills. It became evident to my class teachers that I knew quite a lot about these subjects, well, my Mother had taught me all I knew. Now the teachers had to go one step further, because I was very keen to learn.

In the Domestic Science block was a normal flat. This was meant to give girls an insight into being good housewives. The flat had not been used during the war years because it was too far away from the air raid shelters so it had become a little dilapidated. I was asked to refurbish the bedroom and design a kitchen garden, both tasks I accepted readily.

The bedroom had twin beds for which I made new bedspreads and covered two lampshades. The gardens I would have re-designed if I had been given enough time – but the sewing had taken up a great deal of my time.

I was extremely happy at school and joined the choir and drama class. I took part in all the school plays, Alice in Wonderland and Little Women. I was given the leading part in the Christmas pantomime, I showed no fear of speaking in public or acting out the fool when it was necessary. I longed for my Mother to attend the stage shows but she was still busy with her hospital work and couldn't get time off. I took all things in my stride knowing full well it was all in my challenge, to gain higher places in my class position.

My favourite subjects were needlework (which I could do well) taught by Miss Moore and Mrs. Corcoran. We had a biology teacher by the name of Miss Goodhall. I learned so much from her which has stood me in good stead all my life, how our bodies work and what to eat to make them work better. One day a gentleman brought in a model head made of clear glass. It was set up on the teaching bench. We were told about smoking and what harm it did to our lungs and other parts of our insides. I have never forgotten the black tar that trickled down the throat of the head when the heat machine was switched on. It actually smoked a whole cigarette during our lesson.

A different game came into the playground. It was for older children. We needed to have enough strength in our wrists to flick cigarette cards. These were small cards that fitted into a packet of twenty cigarettes. The idea was to stand several cards against a wall propped up from the ground and from a marked distance away you would flick another card towards the propped up cards and if you knocked it down or covered it you took the card as your prize. The cards became very collectable as they were in sets of topical interest, mainly footballers or cricketers. Some were of birds or animals which brought about another interest in collecting the full set.

A Christmas Pantomime
Jean and Peggy Eyres

I rarely saw Denise these days. She was a year lower than me which made a big difference at that time. I had my own agenda and kept to it. She had made her own friends in her class and no longer needed me. Both of us had gained self confidence from our baby school days which had lead us into a good relationship that would re-kindle from time to time.

I did not like the school dinners. I watched my Mother every Monday morning, fishing about in her purse trying to put together my dinner money. I knew money was short and I felt that I could walk home during the lunch hour, make a sandwich and walk back again. Mum viewed this idea with a little doubt but agreed that if I really didn't like the school dinners it was pointless paying for them. Although it was a long walk there and back at lunchtimes I felt that I was making an effort to help with the living expenses.

Although bread was now rationed, at that time it seemed to me that two slices of bread would not break the bank.

My Mother bought herself a bicycle paid for through the Mutuality man. In hindsight I wonder if she used the dinner money with the hope that I would ride the bicycle to school because I could see no need for her to ride a bicycle. When she bought it, she did in fact ride it for a few weeks but then she decided to let me ride it back and forwards to school. I was pleased with that idea but as it had no gears, I found the ride up hill was a big effort, but riding home down hill was great fun. It had a basket on the front handlebars in which I carried my satchel. I had wheels!

The world stage seemed to have taken on a peaceful phase, but the war in the Far East was still going on. From time to time the newscaster on the radio brought various battles to the fore. Places I had never heard of, but in the Far East two cities came to the notice of everyone around the world. The first Atomic bomb was dropped on Hiroshima with horrific pictures flashed around the world. The one I remember most was of three little girls running towards the camera. They were screaming and without clothes. Little did I realize that their clothes had been blasted off them by the force of the bomb.

We relied on the newspapers to tell us about these events as television was not available until after the war.

My mother and her new bicycle

During the long summer holiday I met up with Denise. We realized that we could venture further away from home now that I had a bicycle and she had a new bicycle. The air raids had all stopped and a peaceful existence was felt by everyone. More varieties of foods were being sold in the shops, although rationing was still with us. We planned to take a picnic and Windsor Castle was to be our destination.

Here were two twelve year olds with big ideas. We decided not to tell anyone of our destination because our Mothers would not have let us go. My Father had driven though Windsor when he took us to Portsmouth, so there was no doubt that I knew the way! Perhaps we would have found the Castle easier if I had remembered that there were no signposts! However, we made our plans and decided that when the weather was fine we would pack up our sandwiches and bottles of lemonade and put them in my bicycle basket.

The day arrived, bright and sunny. My Mother had gone to work and Denise and I set forth upon our mammoth trip. We enjoyed our adventure and within a couple of hours we had a break for lunch. Not eating all our picnic because we didn't know how far we had to go. We were at a place called "Runnymede" which I had read about in our history lessons. King John had signed the Magna Carta here - really? It was an overgrown field by a river! Off we went again, I must admit we did ask directions occasionally but eventually we saw Windsor Castle on the horizon. We were both feeling a little tired and decided that as we could see the Castle that would do for to-day. Next time we could come by bus and stay longer. Before we turned for home I decided to buy a postcard and send it to my Mother because that would be the only way she would believe we had made this journey.

The way home seemed to take for ever but, as we pedalled, we were full of excitement and found extra energy for the last ten miles. When we reached home it was early evening and my Mother was home from work, very agitated but pleased to see me.

"Where the devil have you been? I've been worried to death."

"That's a nice welcome home" I replied. "I've been to Windsor Castle."

"Windsor Castle, do you know how far that is?" she said.

"No, I replied, but it was a long way."

"Thirty five miles there and thirty five miles back. You won't be able to move tomorrow," she said.

"Wow" I replied, "I thought it was a long way, but I wasn't going anywhere tomorrow."

"Or for the rest of the holiday, I'm locking that bicycle away until you go back to school."

And she did, but she gave me a hug when she received my postcard a few days later.

On May 7th 1945. Peace in Europe was declared. The people in the Avenue came out to their front gates to see if it was really true and, when the sound of the Church Bells from across the fields rang peel after peel, we knew it was. There was going to be a huge street party with flags flying from windows and bunting was to be stretched across the roads from bedroom windows. What excitement. Although rationing was still with us, somehow the women found enough of their rations to make cakes and jellies and tasty sandwiches. We had all waited too long for something to celebrate, now we had it. Neighbours shook each other by the hands. Some were shedding tears of relief and happiness. The day of the party dawned. It was a lovely sunny day and the warmth of the sun relaxed us all encouraging us to rejoice in our freedom from war.

I joined the street party in the Cul-de-Sac where Denise lived. I felt that I knew more people there than I did where I lived. We had a great time, balloons and fancy hats were given to us. Each child had a present to take home with them. A colouring book and a few crayons and a fairy cake completed our party.

We had won the war and now we would have to face the aftermath. People were exhausted and weakened by poor diets. Wounded soldiers returning from the battlefields trying to return to their normal way of life in the villages and in the towns, were a constant reminder that most families had either lost a close relative or were facing the trauma of a badly wounded one. I was going to have to face this man I called my Father one day!

A Victory Parade was planned for London. Winston Churchill, the nation's hero was to take the salute in Trafalgar Square before a Royal Air Force fly past over Buckingham Palace when the Royal Family would come out on the Balcony to wave to the crowds. People thronged into London on that day. They all wanted to be part of the celebrations. Flags and banners fluttered in the breeze. Brass bands played the popular tunes of the day and the crowds sang along with them. People climbed on to balconies and even up lampposts. Little did I know at that time, my future husband was one of those who had climbed the lamppost to see Winston Churchill pass by. The hoardings were removed from the lions around Nelson's column in the square and people were climbing all over them. It was a great day for celebration. Most of us had to wait for the Pathe News in the Cinema before we saw the Victory Parade.

The Victory Parade in London
Imperial War Museum N.EA65864

The brown sticky tape came off windows, and when they were cleaned the glass shone.

The black-out curtains came down and the curtains we had not seen for many years went up giving an entirely different aspect to day to day living in the home. The street lights began to come to life, and the late night shopping began again. Although there wasn't much money about people needed to congregate and talk in the evenings. There were no air raid warnings or bombs dropping. We felt safe to walk out at night time again.

CHAPTER NINETEEN
FUN OF THE FAIR

In the spring of 1945, the war was over and a fairground had been arranged for the Whitsun Holiday to be held in Garston Park. It was near the crater left by the V2 rocket which had fallen a few months earlier. The tents and carousel arrived along with the side shows.

Denise and I went to the park as often as we could to keep our eyes on the latest fairground arrival. The carousel had been erected and the horses were all gleaming and bright as if they had been painted up for this special occasion. Perhaps it was the first time in years since they had been on show. There were to be coconut shies (will there be real coconuts?), Denise and I could not remember ever seeing a coconut. Real goldfish swimming in a glass bowl were to be given away as prizes, if you won hoop-la. Roll-a-penny and darts were all there for us to play.

Denise and I didn't have much money so we had to plan our spending. We changed our minds over and over again. We could not wait for Whitsun to arrive. My Mother agreed to come with us and, for a treat, if it was nice weather she planned to take a picnic for us and a blanket to spread on the grass. The day finally came and the sun shone brightly and the clouds were high in the sky. It looked as if it was to be a fine day. We dressed in light weight clothing because it was the month of May. We noticed how short our summer dresses were. We must have grown a lot during this last winter.

We helped to pack the picnic. My Mother was wearing her summer frock which still fitted very well and a straw hat which was years old, but nobody bothered about what people wore those days, and off we went to the park. She held her handbag under her arm (with her treasured ration books and identity cards) and the rug for us to sit on over her arm. Denise and I carried the food with a flask of hot tea and cups to drink it from. We were filled with excitement as we neared the park. The music from the carousel could be heard from a long distance away and seemed to encourage us to walk faster to find a good spot to put the rug down and relax. Everyone was so happy, singing and laughing. It was going to be a great day.

Denise won a gold-fish. I tried hard but couldn't win one. My Mother wanted a ride on the carousel but as we had the picnic basket and rug we couldn't all go on together so Denise and I decided to let Mum go first and we would sit and watch her climb up the stairs and sit on a horse. Her handbag remained under her arm waiting for the music to start. She looked so happy with her straw hat perched on her head. Soon the music started and the horses began to move up and down, slowly at first then they began to gain speed and we could see that she was having difficulty holding everything together. Each time she came round we waved then suddenly her straw hat fell over her eyes and as she moved her hand to push it out of her eyes her handbag flew out of her arms and into the crowd.

Each time she sped round she shouted to us to find her handbag, she thought she had lost her ration books and purse, but we had seen what was happening and we had caught her handbag before it touched the ground. By the time the carousel had stopped she had lost her straw hat as well, but we did eventually manage to find that, not in a very good condition after hundreds of feet had walked over it, but she didn't seem to mind. A hot cup of tea worked wonders and we all agreed that we had had a wonderful afternoon at the fair.

Now that the war was over committees were formed to arrange the official street parties all over the country. Flags flew from windows and flag poles. My Mother had had a flag pole erected in the front garden from which she intended to fly the union Jack on the day my Father was due home but it did fly for the official street party. Bunting stretched across the road from house to house. The food, although still rationed was a little more plentiful and the organizers of the parties came up with extra biscuits and cakes. Mothers made fairy cakes and decorated them in red, white and blue. The wonderful day arrived and the music blared out and children were laughing and shouting and nobody minded at all. Tables and

125

chairs from peoples homes came out into the roads and white tablecloths made from sheets were spread along the tables.

All the children had to take a cup, plate and spoon with their names tied on to the handles just in case they went missing. We all played games and sang songs and ended up with a Conga line which travelled all down the Avenue and up the other side, what a wonderful memory for us all. In the evening after the children had gone home to bed the adults danced in the roads to the music from the gramophone until the early hours of the morning. Next day lots of us took brooms and dustpans out in the streets and swept it all clean. Soon it was all just a memory! I could not believe people could be so friendly to one another except for one knowledgeable gentleman that knocked on our front door. He went to some length to tell my Mother that she had flown the Union Jack upside down and in future she was to get it right. We closed the door and laughed until our sides ached.

"Let that be a lesson to you my darling," she said to me.

*Picture of my Father taken
in Rome, June 1944
Message on the reverse:
To my own darling wife with
the fondest of love
From her adoring husband
Bert xxxx
Italy, June 1944*

My Mother received a lot more letters from my Father now. No censor marks on them these days. He sent us a lovely photograph of himself taken in Italy just after peace had been declared. He was one of the first British soldiers to enter Rome and he was very proud to say that he had seen the Pope in St. Peter's on New Years eve 1944/5. We wondered how long it would be before he actually came home as there were so many troops waiting to get back to their families. Unfortunately the troop ships were held up due to mines floating in the Mediterranean Sea. The minesweepers were kept busy keeping the shipping lanes free for the ships to pass through which made the waiting twice as long.

During the summer of that year my Mother took me back to Portsmouth to visit our relations. Now that the air raids had ceased people were beginning to relax. Although we knew that the war was still being fought in a far away land we, at home, began to feel the need for relaxation. Auntie Betty offered to look after Jimmy for us so off we went to visit our relations.

When we arrived, we were surprised to find the streets still full of rubble, very little had been cleared and it was still difficult to walk on the main roads. There was a shortage of money and councils could not pay to have the streets cleared. It was all going to take time. There was also a shortage of manpower to do the work. The army was still overseas. The men were being brought back slowly. It was a massive job to bring thousands of men back from the war zones. They were being used to clean up the towns and streets where they had been fighting until their time for repatriation arrived.

The trams were running again as the tram lines had been repaired. People needed transport because they couldn't walk along the pavements. We boarded a tram which took us to where my Grandmother's house used to be. Her house was not far from the beach so my Auntie Janet was waiting for us to ask if we would like to go to the beach for a picnic next day with the rest of the family, we could all meet up for a few hours.

We stayed overnight with my other Auntie Helen and her two daughters, Dorothy and Vera. They were both very shy and nervous, which in hindsight could be well understood. They had lived through more bombing raids than I had and they had missed so much schooling. It would be a long time before they forgot their war memories.

We woke up next morning to find the sun shining. We packed up our food supplies for the day and, complete with swimming costumes and towels, we started to walk toward the beach which was not far from Auntie Helen's house. Nearing the beach we realized that we were not going to get near to the sea. Although the water was there so was the barbed wire and barricades. They were all along the shore from Southsea to Eastney and beyond, well over five miles was out of bounds.

We made enquiries as to where we could picnic near the water's edge and we were told to catch the ferry across to Gosport where the Lido had just been re-opened. Wow, a Lido open, that was fantastic! We walked to the ferry which cost one penny each way. As we sailed across the harbour we could see the submarine pens which had been built alongside Portsmouth shipyard. There were also huge anti-aircraft guns sited on Portsdown Hill.

Once we arrived on dry land we had quite a walk to the Lido but when we arrived we felt that we were in a different world. Blue water, little boats bobbing up and down, water slides and a sandy bay for toddlers, but no people, we had the place to ourselves. Lunch was the first thing on our mind, and then we donned our swimming costumes.

We had a rowing boat and the two Aunts took the oars taking us around the lake, then it was our swimming time. I could not swim, neither could my cousins so it was a case of a paddle. My Mother had knitted me a swimming costume in bright yellow with a blue fish on the front. She was very proud of this and displayed me to her sisters. I gingerly went down the steps into the water. Not being able to swim I stayed close to the steps but the water came up to my neck which was exciting until I came to get out of the water. As I climbed up step by step my costume decided to stay down in the water. I was very embarrassed and my Mother ran to cover me with a towel. She retrieved the costume and wrung it out. That was the last time it was ever worn and the memories stayed with me for a long time.

That night I was covered in Calamine lotion as my sunburn was so severe I could not lie on my back. The rest of our short holiday went well and, although I had to keep out of the sun, we made the best of the few days together. We were both pleased to get back home and to be re-united with our little dog Jimmy who licked us all over with pleasure to see us.

CHAPTER TWENTY
THE HOMECOMING

The year was 1946, I was thirteen and the time I had been secretly dreading was drawing closer. One day my Father would arrive. The news readers were telling us daily that the troops were coming home, some by sea others by plane. I knew that it wouldn't be long.

One bright sunny morning, the day I had dreaded arrived. My Mother decided to clean the kitchen floor. This meant that the rag mats were taken up and thrown over the back fence to air. She was singing her usual song, no words that you would understand and the tune was one she had made up in her head, "Every-day, every-day, I love to know," but that was as far as she ever got. Denise used to mimic her and she would ask my Mother, "What happens every day Mrs. Hunt?"

We would all end up laughing. She knew we were cheeky, but we all loved it.

On this particular morning I had finished cleaning the chicken house. This was a job that had to be done every few days especially in the summer months. I heard someone say, "Someone's happy to-day."

The voice was that of a man and it came from the other side of the fence, I looked across and saw a soldier in uniform. It could only have been one man, my Father!

My Mother came running through the kitchen, unlocked the back gate and hugs and kisses went on for some time. I looked on and watched. My feelings were very mixed. I was pleased that he was safe and not injured in any way. I was pleased for my Mother, I knew she had been longing for his return. But, what was going to happen to me? I wanted to run away and hide. A good place would be in the chicken house where it was small and dark. This man was going to alter our comfortable lives. She called me over,

"Jean darling, this is your Daddy," I held out my hand but he put his hands on my shoulders and drew me to himself and kissed me on my cheek. I did not respond. I wondered if he felt my shudder. I went into the kitchen to put the kettle on.

This man was a threat to all I held dear, my Mother and my dog and my way of life!

In any anxious moments, we always put the kettle on!

The floor cleaning was all forgotten. We sat down either side of him as he lit a cigarette. I thought that this was a shame because my Mother had managed to give up her smoking. I looked at his fingers and they were stained dark yellow. Obviously he smoked a lot. He undid his army blouse (his top jacket was called a blouse and it joined his trousers with a webbing belt). He called for me to sit on his lap. I was not keen. I was thirteen years old, grown up, and held an important position in our home. I could hear the kettle singing which was the time for me to go and make the tea. I brought in the cups and saucers. My Father asked if we had a mug for his tea as a cup was not big enough.

"We don't have mugs" I replied.

My Mother chirped up, "I'll get you one for tomorrow."

"Don't bother because I have to go back to my unit to-night to sign off and hand in my kit and uniform. I've come here now to get some clothes to put on so that I can travel back here to stay."

I breathed a sign of relief. My Mother looked all confused.

"What clothes will you take?" she asked.

"Anything I can find to wear from my wardrobe," he replied. "I am going to be given a de-mob suit but it won't be just yet as they can't keep up with the demand at the factories," he said.

He began to untie his kit bag. There were presents for us both which took up most of the space in this canvas bag. He needed the room to put his civilian clothes in as he would return to us out of uniform.

131

First there came pretty scarves for both of us and then he brought out three silk woven wall hangings of Mount Vesuvius erupting. Mum seemed thrilled with them but I couldn't see why. We had no space to hang things like that on our walls! Then it was my turn, more scarves, some stamps from Vatican City for my stamp collection which I was very pleased with and some postcards.

When he was handing out the gifts I noticed his ring. It was very strange. I asked if I could look at it. He laughed, "Do you know what that is?" he asked

"Sort of," I replied.

"When you sent me the photograph of you both with the dog I had it made into a ring."

"But what was the ring made of? " I asked.

"A toothbrush" he laughed.

I sat and thought about that for a while and how clever someone had been to make a ring from a tooth brush.

"Would you like the ring?" he asked "I have no need of it now I am home with you."

"Yes please, did you make it?" I asked.

"No, an Italian prisoner of war found a way of bending the toothbrush handle and by removing the bristles, he formed a space for the miniature photograph, it was then covered with a clear glue to keep it in place."

Taking it off his finger, he handed the ring to me, he thought that he had pleased me. Yes, he had.

He went back to his unit that evening and promised to return within a few days pending the amount of de-mobbing he had to go through in Wiltshire. His kit bag was full of his clothes that had been hanging in his wardrobe for nearly six years. What would he look like the next time we saw him?

A few days later he did return to us. This time the Union Jack, right way up, was flying from the flag pole in the front garden. Everyone knew my Father was home. The neighbours all came in to welcome him. It was a time for friendship and happiness exchanging memories and making plans for the future.

The first night he had come home to stay he took me to one side and said, "Now that I am home, you have to move into the back bedroom."

I didn't like that. I went to my Mother and complained bitterly.

"Your Father is home now and his place is in his bedroom with me. You can have your own bedroom in the back room. We must do what he wants."

"But I've always slept in your bed," I said. "I have always looked after you"

"Yes you have been a very good girl and a great help to me," she replied. "Your Father has returned and now he will look after both of us."

I was furious. How dare this man come into our home and throw me out of my Mother's bed. I'd been the one looking after her while he was away all those years. I had a firm dislike of this man. Next morning I threw their feather bed out of the window complete with pillows, sheets and blankets and ran off to tell Denise what I had done. He had come home from one war and started another

All service personnel were to be given a complete set of new clothes. As yet, many of them had not started work to earn enough to buy these items. They would need clothing coupons, so the Government gave them enough clothes to live with until they all went back to their jobs. Many of them had no jobs to go back to. So many factories and places of work had been bombed. It was a case of starting all over again.

*Demob clothes issued
to military personnel*

*Imperial War Museum
N.CH18629*

FEWER SUITS IN COMING YEAR

EFFECT OF QUICKER DEMOBILISATION

A warning that the speed-up in demobilisation meant fewer clothes for men was given by Sir Stafford Cripps, President of the Board of Trade, at a luncheon of outfitters in London, yesterday.

"A large proportion of the total production of men's outer wear has to be diverted to the Ministry of Supply for use by our demobilised men." he said.

In the latter half of 1944 the Ministry of Supply agreed to aim at a target of 35,000 suits a week for demobilisation purposes. This figure was very rarely approached, and latterly it had fallen off during the holiday season and the VE and VJ celebrations.

To meet the requirements of the faster rate of releases they would require 75,000 suits a week for the rest of this year and 65,000 during 1946.

NO INCREASE NEXT YEAR

"Supplies of men's clothing cannot possibly increase to any extent above the present level during the next year," said Sir Stafford. "The public pressed very hard for increased demobilisation. Now they will have to sacrifice something for it by not expecting more men's clothes for a while.'

As the weekly total output of ready-made suits was only a little over 100,000 a week, the outlook for civilians might seem to be very dark. The picture was lightened by the return to the clothing industry of men at the rate of 1,000 a week on the average since October, 1944. Recently the figure has reached 2,000 a week.

In addition to the output of ready-made suits, 60,000 jackets and 150,000 trousers a week were produced. The output of bespoke suits was believed to be about 25,000 a week.

During the next year about 1,000,000 overcoats and 3,000,000 waterproofs would be required for released men.

"The urgent need for exports and the absolutely essential demands of demobilisation must come first, and are bound to diminish our capacity to return to a full and free market for the ordinary civilians."

My Father was fortunate enough to have his place of work waiting for his return. So many men from the printing works had been killed in the war and when he went back on night work it was only for a short while. He was promoted to managerial status and began to live life in the normal way, working from eight in the morning until six in the evening. We began to live as a family again, well that's how it looked from the outside. I was still rebellious and my Mother knew she had a problem with me.

My Father took me in hand and tried punishing me for throwing the bedding out of the window. I was not to receive pocket money and my outings with Denise were strictly monitored, which, of course, made things worse. In hindsight, my Mother should have made an effort to separate me when peace was declared and I should have been in my own bedroom long before my Father came home. She had had enough time for me to become adapted to a new way of life. I was at the wrong age to be slighted in the way I was. I can understand now how it all happened but, at that time, my life with my Father was far from a happy one.

I can see him now in my memory, in his de-mob suit. It was a light grey pin stripe with baggy trousers and wide lapels on the jacket. He was also given a wide brimmed trilby hat! He did not like the suit and I made matters worse by laughing at him describing him as 'Spiv,' making reference to Arthur English the comedian who wore exactly the same clothes as my Father. My Mother took me to one side and gave me a good talking to.

"Don't you laugh at him. He is finding it hard enough to try and adjust to civilian life."

I should have kept quiet and curbed my tongue but instead it was 'fuel to the fire'.

The national workforce of men was depleted. Women were now in the front line of employment. Gone were the days of wives and mothers staying at home. Not any more, they were out there alongside the men, earning enough to keep themselves and their families. Whole families were re-located. Where workers were needed the women went and their families went too.

New towns were to be built, from what, before the war, were small villages. The country's infrastructure was being rebuilt from the rubble. New ideas were being tried out. Rationing still continued, but now that my Father was home we had a bigger allowance each week and more items were coming into the shops which didn't need ration books.

Soon the Austin Seven came off the blocks and stood on the ground once more ready for it's first journey for several years. My Mother's loving care was rewarded, as it shone beautifully when the polish was applied. My Father decided that we should go on holiday before he started back to work. We were to visit his Mother and Father. Their house in Finsbury Park had been demolished by a bomb so they were forced into making a move and, as my Grandfather no longer worked in London, they went to Portsmouth to live nearer his sister.

The Austin 7

My Father tried to placate me by inviting Denise to come on holiday with us. I ran like the wind across the road to ask her if she would like to come to Portsmouth with us in the car. She jumped up and down with delight. So it was that we were off on holiday in 1947 at the age of fourteen, all in the brightly polished Austin Seven.

We all slept in my Grandmother's house. There were two bedrooms in this small house. My parents slept on a put-you-up in the front room downstairs. Denise and I shared a double bed upstairs while my Grandparents slept in their own room. Jimmy slept in the kitchen.

Mum and Dad together again

We were now of an age when we could go off on our own. We enjoyed that freedom and responded well to it. There was a draper's shop not too far away and with a little money in our pocket we did some shopping. We had pleasure in buying a length of material, enough for two blouses, together with needles and threads, a piece of lace trimming and a length of ribbon. We went back to my Grandma's house and borrowed her scissors and cut out two blouses, one for me and the other for Denise. There was no sewing machine available so we sewed by hand enjoying every moment. The next day our blouses were ready to wear. It was with great pride that we walked out that afternoon wearing our new hand made blouses.

Jean and Denise

Because we had behaved so well my Father decided that we would go on holiday again in the summer. This time we had to consider the dog. We had taken him everywhere since his return but we knew we could not take him on holiday for a week. My Father wrote to his army pal who had returned from Italy to live in London with his wife Tess, asking them if they would like to come and stay in our house for their holiday and whether they would look after Jimmy. Their answer was yes, they would love to stay in our house away from all the rubble and cleaning up that was going on in London. To live in a house in the country would be a pleasure as they lived in a flat just off Oxford Street so the dates were arranged and we began to plan our holiday.

This time it was to be Butlins at Skegness. Wow, that was so exciting. Denise was able to come with me and we really lit up the town. We joined in everything, stayed up late, met a couple of boys and the four of us had a wonderful week. After the holiday I began to get on with my Father a lot better. His problem, I considered, was that he could not forget that I had grown up during those years he was away. Maybe he thought I would stay the little seven year old girl he had left behind when he went to war. Or perhaps he didn't want me to grow up, but whatever it was, both of us had a job adjusting.

CHAPTER TWENTY ONE
WORK IN PROGRESS

I was now in my fourteenth year and big decisions lay ahead for me. When I was asked over the years what I would like to be when I grew up the answer was always the same, a nurse! I knew when I hadn't sat the eleven plus examination that I would not be accepted for a State Registered Nurse because I hadn't recieved a Grammar School education.

Although this was not entirely my fault, I would have to accept that decision for the rest of my life. I also knew that there were variations of nursing careers that I could have pursued. With a little help and advice, I was willing to work for the qualifications and I knew that given half the chance I would gain the achievement in the end. However, my parents had other ideas. Neither of them wanted me to leave home and, to get a nursing qualification, it would mean that I would have to 'live in' whilst training. So when we actually got down to talking about my future employment, nursing wasn't even on the agenda!

We were approaching the winter of 1947. The summer had not been good and the farmers could not get the harvest in until late September. The potato harvest was abysmal, the rains came and the farmers could not lift the crops from the fields. As I was in the last year of my schooling I was asked by The Headmistress if I would go on the farms to pick potatoes. I agreed. This was the chance I needed, to see what work was like – I soon realized that school was the better option!

An Army truck stood at the entrance to the school playground and all the fourteen year old girls were put in the truck and driven out into the countryside. Foggy weather hung over the area which meant the drizzle drenched us all day. We were wet through and by the time three o'clock came we were all ready to get into that truck and back to school. I ached so much from bending down all day, I thought that I would never be straight again. The next day the truck came and off we went to the farm again to finish off what we had started the previous day. One thing that kept us going was the promise of getting paid for the work. Four shillings a day – big money for a fourteen year old!

The weather worsened and in December the temperatures dropped and the snow came. Denise and I were walking to and from school each day because the snow was so deep we couldn't ride our bicycles. Along the roadside the snow lay two feet deep so it came over the top of our Wellington boots. We had to take a spare pair of socks to change into when we arrived at school and our wet ones hung over the school radiators along with everyone else's, but at least they were warm to put on before we started to walk the two miles back home.

I was ready to leave school in the December and start work but Parliament raised the school leaving age to fifteen. I had to stay at school for another year. I was ready to leave tomorrow!

My end of term report showed that I had achieved my goal after the years of hard work. I had come 4th in my class examinations. I was thrilled, thinking back to that very first class I was put in on my first day at that school , what an achievement. Now I had a whole year to worry about the plans my parents had in mind for me.

During the snowy period the temperatures fell so low that new records had been set in the meteorology charts. The snow had turned to ice. Whole fields of snow looked like the Artic, it cracked when you trod on it. Trains stopped running, and driving became impossible. Although food was becoming easier to get, rationing still continued. The snow drifts meant that trucks which transported it could not get the food to the shops!

The bad weather stayed with us until May the following year.

In the summer of 1948 I left school and, after a couple of weeks' holiday, I started work, not as a nurse, but as a clerk in the office of the printing factory where my Father worked. I was not happy about this and I felt that he was still watching over me. One day I would escape from his world and find my own way but life was acceptable for the present. Denise had to stay on at school until the following year but we were still the best of friends. Our lives were to take different paths. She started work in the Cashier's Office in the Town Hall offices in 1949 but that's a different story!

Addendum

Seventy years on, a husband, two daughters and two grandchildren later, I find myself living in a quiet Lincolnshire village. Now a widow, I have had time to reflect on my early days. Life has moved on at an alarming rate, technology allows us to see each other in a hand held mobile 'phone amongst other things. I have seen the need to keep the past in the present and to allow future generations to read and talk about "How it used to be".

Denise is still my dearest friend and has been an inspiration to me. I was always the instigator and she followed, sometimes she would issue words of caution.

Whilst doing my research I have been amazed at the coincidences that have come to light:-. Whilst visiting R.A.F Coningsby Visitors Centre, home of the Lancaster Bomber, I was shown around by Jim Balsom, a R.A.F ex-serviceman, now a guide at the centre. We exchanged war experiences and it came to light that he was in Southsea the day of the raid on Dieppe and, like me, he now lives in Lincolnshire. He listened to my story of the dog fight and how I missed getting my bullet, he put his hand in his pocket and drew out a spent bullet and gave it to me. It meant so much, after all these years I had my keepsake.

A further co-incidence came recently in the obituary column of our local Parish Newsletter. The passing of a local resident Margaret Templeman had also collected for Mrs. Churchill's Aid to Russia Fund, just as I had some 175 miles away.

The crashing of a Lancaster Bomber on the 4th of October 1943 has been documented by our local historian Mr. David Barnett. The young pilot, Capt. Thomas H. Morgan, DFC from British Columbia was killed whilst flying the aircraft after it had been serviced ready to return to bombing missions. The aircraft fell into our Village Square and several houses were damaged. His photograph, together with that of a Memorial Stone which now stands in the Village Square, for the crew who were killed that day, is a sobering memory for us all.